P9-DCX-250

GRADES 3-5

Mathematics Assessment Sampler

Mathematics Assessment Samplers

A series edited by Anne M. Collins

GRADES 3-5

Mathematics Assessment Sampler

Items Aligned with NCTM's
Principles and Standards for School Mathematics

Jane D. Gawronski, *Editor*
San Diego State University, San Diego, California

Anne M. Collins, *Series Editor*
Boston College Mathematics Institute, Chestnut Hill, Massachusetts

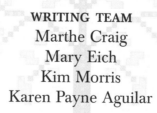

WRITING TEAM
Marthe Craig
Mary Eich
Kim Morris
Karen Payne Aguilar

NATIONAL COUNCIL OF
TEACHERS OF MATHEMATICS

Copyright © 2005 by
THE NATIONAL COUNCIL OF TEACHERS OF MATHEMATICS, INC.
1906 Association Drive, Reston, VA 20191-1502
All rights reserved

Library of Congress Cataloging-in-Publication Data

Mathematics assessment sampler, grades 3–5 : items aligned with NCTM's principles and standards for school mathematics / Jane D. Gawronski, editor ; writing team, Marthe Craig ... [et al.].
        p. cm. – (Mathematics assessment samplers)
    Includes bibliographical references.
    ISBN 0-87353-579-0
1. Mathematics–Study and teaching (Elementary)   2.   Mathematical ability–Testing.
I. Gawronski, J. D. II. Craig, Marthe. III. Series.
    QA11.2.M2775 2005
    372.7–dc22

                                                                2005003488

The National Council of Teachers of Mathematics is a public voice of mathematics education, providing vision, leadership, and professional development to support teachers in ensuring mathematics learning of the highest quality for all students.

The publications of the National Council of Teachers of Mathematics present a variety of viewpoints. The views expressed or implied in this publication, unless otherwise noted, should not be interpreted as official positions of the Council.

PRINTED IN THE UNITED STATES OF AMERICA

Contents

On the Cover

The term *sampler* comes from the Latin *exemplum*, meaning "an example to be followed, a pattern, a model or example." The earliest known samplers date to the sixteenth century, although samplers were probably stitched long before that time. Beginning in the mid–eighteenth century, young girls commonly worked samplers as part of their education. During Victorian times, samplers metamorphosed into decorative articles hung by proud parents on parlor walls. As designs became more elaborate, generally only one stitch remained in use, leading to the well–known cross–stitch samplers of today.

The electronically "stitched" sampler on the cover highlights the relationships among knowledge (owl), learning (school), and the NCTM Standards (logo). The number patterns (Fibonacci sequence, counting sequence) embedded in the border design echo pattern motifs seen in samplers in earlier times.

The Mathematics Assessment Samplers are intended to give teachers examples— not exhaustive listings—of assessment items that reveal what students know and can do in mathematics, that pinpoint areas of strengths and weakness in students' mathematical knowledge, and that shape teachers' curricular and instructional decisions toward the goal of maximizing all students' understanding of mathematics.

Preface

The National Council of Teachers of Mathematics asked our task force to compile a list of assessment items that support *Principles and Standards for School Mathematics* (NCTM 2000). This book, one of four in the series, focuses on classroom assessment in grades 3–5. The other three books, for teachers in prekindergarten–grade 2, grades 6–8, and grades 9–12, also contain practical examples and samples of student work aligned with the NCTM Standards. Each of the books contains multiple-choice, short-response, and extended-response questions designed to help classroom teachers identify problems specifically related to certain of the NCTM Standards and Expectations. Matrices with this information are contained in the appendix.

NCTM's *Assessment Standards for School Mathematics* (1995) tells us that classroom assessment should—

- provide a rich variety of mathematical topics and problem situations;
- give students opportunities to investigate problems in many ways;
- question and listen to students;
- look for evidence of learning from many sources;
- expect students to use concepts and procedures effectively in solving problems.

Our collection of examples was compiled from many sources including state and provincial assessments. We know that standardized assessment has a major impact on what educators do in the classroom. Because most formal assessments include multiple-choice items, we have included them in this Sampler. Owing to the limited amount of information to be gleaned from most multiple-choice items, we have added an "explain your thinking," "justify your solution," or "how do you know?" component to most multiple-choice items. We believe that if students are going to be prepared to answer multiple-choice questions on formal assessments, they need classroom experience in answering this type of item, but we also want to be sure that students can support their answers by showing their work.

We have included a variety of rubrics as examples of how extended-response questions might be scored. We believe that students who know in advance how their answers will be evaluated will strive to meet the expected criteria; we realize, however, that for many assessment instruments, students are not privileged to this information. For classroom assessment, though, we believe that students should be given the rubric as a component of the assessment.

We encourage you to use these items with your students and hope that you find the bibliography and resources sections useful as you work toward extending your own classroom repertoire of assessment items.

Acknowledgments

The editors and writing team wish to thank the educators listed below for their suggestions, contributions of student work, reviews, and general assistance.

Lori Albers

Kim Anderson

Frances Basich-Whitney

Jennie M. Bennett

Barbara Bidlingmaier

Cathy Boyle

Rick Callan

Bill Collins

Janie Dubé

Jennifer Emmett

Michael Feldstein

Pek Hu Liu

Mike Klass

Steve Klass

Mike Maxon

Liz Page

Linda Scheffield

Janet Springfield

About This Series

An emphasis on assessment, testing, and gathering evidence of student achievement has become an educational phenomenon in recent years. In fact, we can fairly say that assessment is driving many educational decisions, including grade placement, graduation, and teacher evaluation. With that influence in mind, educators need to use good assessment material as an essential tool in the teaching and learning processes. Good problems are those that are mathematically rich, can be solved in multiple ways, promote critical thinking, and can be evaluated in a consistent manner—that is, teacher X and teacher Y would be likely to evaluate a problem in the same manner with the appropriate rubric.

Assessment is actually only one of three major considerations in the processes of teaching and learning. As such, assessment must be viewed in conjunction with curriculum and instruction. Just as a curriculum aligned with standards can guide instruction, so too can assessment guide both instructional and curricular decisions. Therefore, items designed to assess specific standards and expectations should be incorporated into the classroom repertoire of assessment tasks.

In its *Assessment Standards for School Mathematics* (*Assessment Standards*), the National Council of Teachers of Mathematics (NCTM 1995) articulated four purposes for assessments and their results: (1) monitoring students' progress toward learning goals, (2) making instructional decisions, (3) evaluating students' achievement, and (4) evaluating programs. Further, the Assessment Principle in *Principles and Standards for School Mathematics* (*Principles and Standards*) states that "assessment should not merely be done to students; rather it should be done for students" (NCTM 2000, p. 22). We have included a variety of rubrics in this series to assist the classroom teacher in providing feedback to students. Often, if students understand what is expected of them on individual extended-response problems, they tend to answer the questions more fully or provide greater detail than when they have no idea about the grading rubric being used.

This series was designed to present samples of student assessment items aligned with *Principles and Standards* (NCTM 2000). The items reflect the mathematics that all students should know and be able to do in grades prekindergarten–2, 3–5, 6–8, and 9–12. The items focus both on students' conceptual knowledge and on their procedural skills. The problems were designed as formative assessments, that is, assessments that help teachers learn how their students think about mathematical concepts, how students' understanding is communicated, and how such evidence can be used to guide instructional decisions.

The sample items contained in this publication are not a comprehensive set of examples but, rather, just a sampling. The problems are suitable for use as benchmark assessments or as evaluations of how well students have met particular NCTM Standards and Expectations. Some student work is included with comments so that teachers can objectively examine a particular problem; study the way a student responded; and draw conclusions that, we hope, will translate into classroom practice.

This series also contains a chapter for professional development. This chapter was developed with preservice, in-service, and professional development staff in mind. It addresses the idea that by examining students' thinking, teachers can gain insight into what instruction is necessary to move students forward in developing mathematical proficiency. In other words, assessment can drive instructional decisions.

NCTM's *Assessment Standards* (1995) indicates that (a) assessment should enhance mathematics learning, (b) assessment should promote equity, (c) assessment should be an open process, (d) assessment should promote valid inferences about mathematics learning, and (e) assessment should be a coherent process. This series presents problems and tasks that, when used as one component of the assessment process, help meet those Assessment Standards.

Introduction: About This Book

THIS sampler provides the classroom teacher with samples of assessment items for grades 3–5 that are specifically and purposely aligned with the recommendations in NCTM's *Principles and Standards for School Mathematics* (*Principles and Standards*) (NCTM 2000). Classifying an item as targeting a particular Expectation was not always a easy task, because many of the Expectations are interrelated. Often, a good assessment problem assesses multiple Expectations from across the strands. The editors and writing team tried to classify each item on the basis of the Expectation that seemed to us to be the "best fit" for the item. The Content and Process Standards addressed by the assessment items are indicated in the items matrices in the appendix.

We have selected the sample assessment items from some state assessments, the Nova Scotia Elementary Mathematics Program Assessment, the National Assessment of Educational Progress, and the Third International Study of Science and Mathematics, as well as from the private sector. Additionally, we have included original items to complete the collection. In selecting items matched with the NCTM Standards, we have deliberately chosen assessment formats that are most widely found on state assessments: multiple choice, short response, and extended response.

Students are being assessed at the state level with a preponderance of multiple-choice items, so we have chosen samples of multiple-choice items that we think have the potential to help teachers make informed instructional decisions. The distractors that students choose in answering multiple-choice items can often foster insights into students' misconceptions. Moreover, correct and incorrect responses to multiple-choice items can supply teachers with information that is useful in planning instruction.

We have included "teacher notes" to suggest ways to make multiple-choice items more meaningful, either (a) by asking students to justify their answers or explain their choices or (b) by removing the distractors, requiring students to produce the solution and justify their answers. We have also made suggestions for altering, extending, or modifying some of the items.

We have also included short-answer and extended-response items designed to give students the opportunity to demonstrate their skills and understanding in a less restrictive format. We believe that an important outcome of assessment is to determine how well students are able to communicate mathematically and how fluent they are in using multiple representations, skills that are better assessed in non-multiple-choice formats. Asking students to identify their problem-solving strategies and to justify their reasoning are ways in which the classroom teacher can determine the necessary next steps for subsequent mathematics lessons.

We hope that you find this compilation of problems and items interesting and helpful in examining your students' proficiency in attaining the Standards and Expectations and in identifying those areas in which they need more opportunities to explore the mathematics involved.

Additionally, we hope that you use this material to learn about your students' thinking and consider how your students' responses might guide your instruction. We have designed the professional development chapter to give examples of how students' responses can lend insight into their thinking and can indicate how diverse their thinking really is. We hope that the professional development chapter will be used by both in-service and preservice teachers as well as by professional development providers as we work together to understand students' thinking and to use that information to make more effective instructional decisions.

1

Number and Operations

When students leave grade 5, they should be able to solve problems involving whole-number computation and should recognize that each operation will help them solve many different types of problems. They should be able to solve many problems mentally, to estimate a reasonable result for a problem, to efficiently recall or derive the basic number combinations for each operation, and to compute fluently with multidigit whole numbers. They should understand the equivalence of fractions, decimals, and percents and the information each type of representation conveys. With these understandings and skills, they should be able to develop strategies for computing with familiar fractions and decimals.[1]

In grades 3–5, students should use communication as a tool for understanding and generating solution strategies. Their writing should be more coherent than in earlier grades, and their increasing mathematical vocabulary can be used along with everyday language to explain concepts. Depending on the purpose for writing, such as taking notes or writing to explain an answer, students' descriptions of problem-solving strategies and reasoning should become more detailed and coherent.[2]

In grades 3–5, students need to develop and use a variety of representations of mathematical ideas to model problem situations, to investigate mathematical relationships, and to justify or disprove conjectures. They should use informal representations, such as drawings, to highlight various features of problems; they should use physical models to represent and understand ideas such as multiplication and place value. They should also learn to use equations, charts, and graphs to model and solve problems. These representations serve as tools for thinking about and solving problems. They also help students communicate their thinking to others. Students in these grades will use both external models—ones that they can build, change, and inspect—as well as mental images.[3]

—National Council of Teachers of Mathematics

---

1 National Council of Teachers of Mathematics (2000, p. 149)
2 National Council of Teachers of Mathematics (2000, p. 194)
3 National Council of Teachers of Mathematics (2000, p. 206)

THE ASSESSMENT tasks in this strand are designed to illuminate students' understanding of the concepts recommended by the NCTM Number and Operation Standards for grades 3–5 and students' ability to use the targeted skills to successfully solve problems. In addition, the open-response questions offer teachers the opportunity to assess students' ability to communicate mathematical concepts in writing and to represent mathematical ideas in a variety of forms.

Number and Operations Assessment Items

Standard: Understand numbers, ways of representing numbers, relationships among numbers, and number systems

Expectation: Understand the place-value structure of the base-ten number system and be able to represent and compare whole numbers and decimals

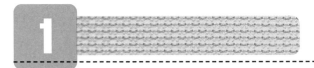

I am a number. When you switch the digit in the ten thousands place with the digit in the hundreds place, I become 795,062. What number am I?

> **Teacher note:** This item can be adapted to make additional items. The number and place values can easily be changed to make new items.
> **About the mathematics:** This item requires an understanding of place value in a nonroutine context.
> **Solution:** 705,962

2

Some of the animals at the zoo were weighed. Which list shows the animals from the heaviest to the lightest?

Animal	Weight in Pounds
Elephant	7243
Rhinoceros	3869
Hippopotamus	5319
Walrus	3209

a. Elephant, hippopotamus, walrus, rhinoceros
b. Walrus, rhinoceros, hippopotamus, elephant
c. Hippopotamus, elephant, rhinoceros, walrus
d. Elephant, hippopotamus, rhinoceros, walrus

About the mathematics: This item requires the ability to compare and order four-digit numbers.
Solution: d

3

Write a decimal that represents the shaded part of the figure.

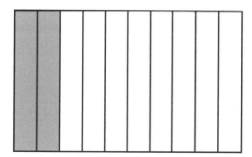

Source: Adapted from National Assessment of Educational Progress (1990, block 4M7, item 18)

About the mathematics: Students demonstrate the ability to interpret a graphic representation of a decimal.

Solution: 0.2

Standard: Understand numbers, ways of representing numbers, relationships among numbers, and number systems

Expectation: Recognize equivalent representations for the same number and generate them by decomposing and composing numbers

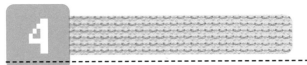

Which of the following does not equal 873?

a. 8 hundreds, 73 ones
b. 8 hundreds, 73 tens
c. 87 tens, 3 ones
d. 8 hundreds, 7 tens, 3 ones

About the mathematics: This item requires an understanding of place value and a recognition of equivalent expressions for three-digit numbers.

Solution: b

Standard: Understand numbers, ways of representing numbers, relationships among numbers, and number systems

Expectation: Develop understanding of fractions as parts of unit wholes, as parts of a collection, as locations on number lines, and as divisions of whole numbers

5

Which point is incorrectly labeled on the number line shown below?

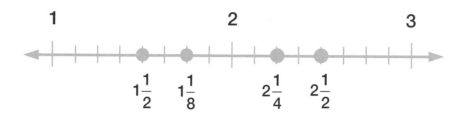

Justify your answer.

Source: Adapted from the Massachusetts Comprehensive Assessment System, Grade 4, Mathematics (release of spring 2002 test items, item 19)

About the mathematics: This item calls for an understanding of relative size of unit fractions as parts of mixed numbers, and of fractions as locations on the number line.

Solution: $1\frac{1}{8}$ is incorrectly labeled. The explanation should clearly demonstrate the understanding that $1\frac{1}{8}$ is less than $1\frac{1}{2}$ by referencing the relative size of the denominators.

6

Think carefully about the following question. Write a complete answer. You may use drawings, words, and numbers to explain your answer. Be sure to show all your work.

José ate $\frac{1}{2}$ of a pizza.
Ella ate $\frac{1}{2}$ of another pizza.
José said that he ate more pizza than Ella, but Ella said they both ate the same amount. Use words and pictures to show that Jose could be right.

Source: National Assessment of Educational Progress (1992, block 4M7, item 10)

About the mathematics: This item requires an understanding that the size of the whole determines the size of the parts.

Solution: José may have been correct if his pizza was larger than Ella's. The size of the whole determines whether he ate more than, less than, or the same as Ella.

Student Work

Correct Student Response

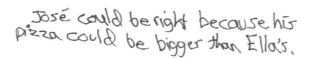

Satisfactory Student Responses

Both students showed two different-sized pizzas, but neither provided an explanation.

Response 1   Response 2

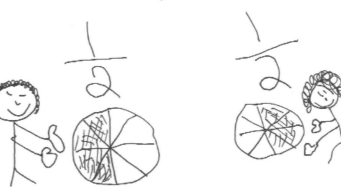

Partially Correct Student Response

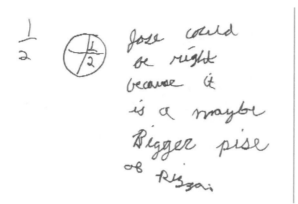

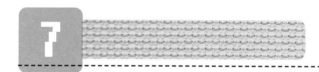

Jose could be right because it is a maybe Bigger pise of Pizza

Incorrect or Off-Task Student Response

Jose ate ½

7

Jennifer is making a number line for fractions between 0 and 1. At which point should she put $^1/_2$? At which point should she put $^7/_8$?

About the mathematics: This item calls for an understanding of fractions as locations on the number line, and the ability to compare and order fractions.
Solutions: D, F

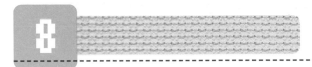

If is $^1/_2$ of a unit, then draw 1 unit.

About the mathematics: Students demonstrate their understanding of representations of fractions, of equivalent fractions, and of fractions as parts of a collection.

Solution:  **or**

If  is 1 unit, then  is _____.

About the mathematics: Students demonstrate their understanding of representations of fractions, of equivalent fractions, and of fractions as parts of a collection.
Solution: $^2/_3$ unit

Students in Mrs. Johnson's class were asked to tell why $^4/_5$ is greater than $^2/_3$. Whose reason is best? Explain your answer.

a. Kelly said, "Because 4 is greater than 2."
b. Keri said, "Because 5 is larger than 3."
c. Kim said, "Because $^4/_5$ is closer to 1 than $^2/_3$."
d. Kevin said, "Because 4 + 5 is more than 2 + 3."

> **Source:** Adapted from National Assessment of Educational Progress (1990, block 4M7, item 15)
>
> **About the mathematics:** This item requires an understanding of the meaning of numerator and denominator, and the use of benchmarks to determine the size of fractions.
>
> **Solution:** c

On a number line, 0.6 is closest to which of the following:

$$^1/_4, \quad ^1/_2, \quad \text{or} \quad 1?$$

Justify your answer.

About the mathematics: Students demonstrate an understanding of the meaning of numerator and denominator, and depending on the explanation, the ability to use models, benchmarks, or equivalent forms to judge the size of fractions.

Solution: $^1/_2$. The explanation should demonstrate the use of models, benchmarks, or equivalent forms to compare fractions or could explain that 0.5 is one-half and that 0.6 is just a little bit larger.

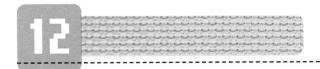

Which of the following represent 0.4?

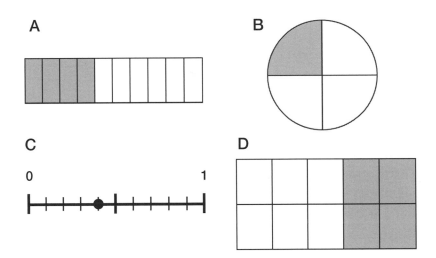

How do you know?

Source: Adapted from Massachusetts Comprehensive Assessment System, Grade 4, Mathematics (release of spring 2002 test items, item 34)

About the mathematics: This item requires an understanding of the meaning of numerator and denominator, and the ability to use models to judge the size of fractions.

Solution: A, C, D. The explanation should indicate that A, C, and D show four parts of ten, whereas B shows one part of four.

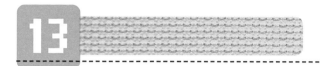

Answer the following question about this fraction:

$$\frac{23}{?}$$

If this fraction is just a little more than 1, what would [?] be?

Source: Nova Scotia Elementary Mathematics Program Assessment (2003, item 5)

About the mathematics: To be successful, students must understand the meaning of numerator and denominator.

Solution: Any number between 20 and 22 is acceptable.

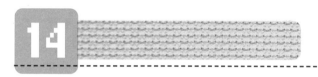

Which circle has approximately the same fraction shaded as that of the rectangle?

About the mathematics: This problem connects two common visual representations of fractions, the rectangle and the circle.

Solution: (D) The rectangle has $^{10}/_{18}$ boxes shaded; this amount is slightly more than half. The only circle with slightly more than half shaded is D.

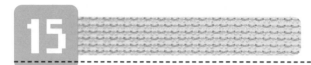

15

Five students are sharing a pizza. Rhonda decides she doesn't want any and says she will give her share to Ivan. Ivan told the teacher, "I get two pieces of pizza." The teachers said, "If Rhonda doesn't want any, I'll just cut the pizza into four pieces."

a) What fraction of the pizza would Ivan get using his plan?
b) What fraction will he get using his teacher's plan?
c) Who gets Rhonda's share under the teacher's plan?
d) Whose plan gives Ivan more pizza?
e) How do you know? Show your reasoning using pictures or words.

Source: Adapted from Cynthia Lanius's Lessons, "Who Wants Pizza?—Part 3" (math.rice.edu/~lanius/fractions/frac3.html)

About the mathematics: This item requires an understanding of relative size of fractions. Depending on the explanation in (e), it requires the ability to use models, benchmarks, and equivalent forms to judge the size of fractions.

Solution

a) $^2/_5$ of the pizza
b) $^1/_4$ of the pizza
c) Each of the four remaining students gets $^1/_4$ of Rhonda's share.
d) Ivan's plan gives Ivan more pizza.
e) In Ivan's plan, he gets $^2/_5$ of a pizza. In the teacher's plan, he gets $^1/_4$ of a pizza.

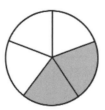

Ivan's plan

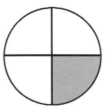

Teacher's plan

Standard: Understand numbers, ways of representing numbers, relation-ships among numbers, and number systems

Expectation: Recognize and generate equivalent forms of commonly used fractions, decimals, and percents

16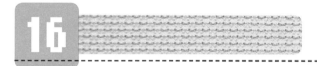

Which shaded region(s) show fractions equivalent to $2/3$?

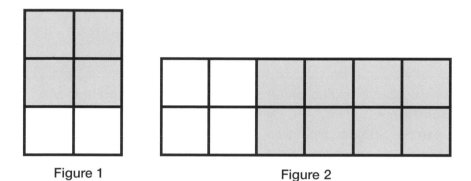

Figure 1   Figure 2

a. Figure 1 only
b. Figure 2 only
c. Both figure 1 and figure 2
d. Neither figure 1 nor figure 2

Source: Nova Scotia Elementary Mathematics Program Assessment (2003, item 5)

Teacher note: Students could be asked to draw other figures showing frac-tions equivalent to $2/3$, and to explain how they know that the fractions are equivalent.

About the mathematics: Students must be able to use models to judge the size of fractions, and to recognize equivalent forms of commonly used fractions.

Solution: c

Mrs. Washington asked her students what fractional part of these 12 circles is shaded.

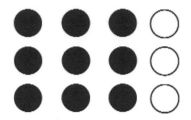

Odessa thinks the answer is $^9/_{12}$.

Bob thinks the answer is $^3/_4$.

a. Who is correct—Odessa, Bob, or both or neither?
b. Write an explanation to Odessa and Bob about how you figured out your answer. Draw your own pictures to go with your explanation.

> **Source:** Adapted from Kentucky Department of Education, Grade 5, Mathematics (January 2004, sample released items, item 5: "A Fractional Part")
>
> **About the mathematics:** Students must recognize equivalent forms of $^3/_4$, and give reasons why they are equivalent.
>
> **Solution:** They are both right.
> Odessa thinks the answer is $^9/_{12}$ because she counted nine circles shaded out of twelve altogether.
> Bob thinks the answer is $^3/_4$ because he counted three columns shaded out of four altogether.

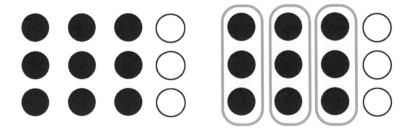

The same number of circles are shaded no matter which fraction you use.

18

Express the area of the shaded region of each drawing as a percent of the whole drawing.

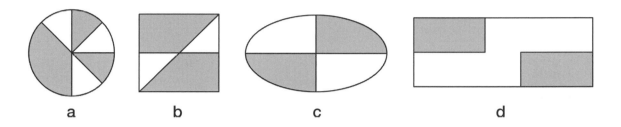

a   b   c   d

About the mathematics: This item requires students to identify percents as parts of wholes visually.

Solution

    a. 62.5%
    b. 75%
    c. 50%
    d. 40%

Teacher note: Students could be asked to explain how they determined the percents.

Standard: Understand numbers, ways of representing numbers, relationships among numbers, and number systems

Expectation: Explore numbers less than 0 by extending the number line and through familiar applications

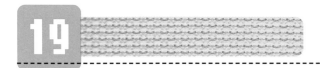

The table shows the temperature on four winter mornings in the Berkshire Mountains.

**Winter Temperatures
in the Berkshire Mountains**

Day	Temperature at 6:00 A.M.
Thursday	–9° C
Friday	–10° C
Saturday	–18° C
Sunday	–12° C

Which day had the warmest morning?

a. Thursday
b. Friday
c. Saturday
d. Sunday

Source: Massachusetts Comprehensive Assessment System: Grade 6, Mathematics (release of spring 2002 test items, item 16)
About the mathematics: To solve this item, students must understand relative values of numbers less than 0 in the context of temperature.
Solution: a

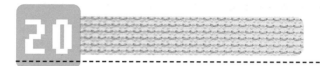

Corina was investigating information about natural wonders of the world.

- She found that Mount Everest is the highest mountain in the world. It is 29,028 feet ABOVE sea level.
- She found that the Marianas Trench in the Pacific Ocean is the lowest point on earth. It is 35,840 BELOW sea level.

a. If Corina could throw a rock from the top of Mount Everest to the bottom of the Marianas Trench, how many feet would it fall?
b. Draw a diagram, and explain your answer for part a.

Source: Kentucky Mathematics, Form 4a, Grade 5 (sample released items 1998–1999, item 10)

About the mathematics: This item requires an understanding of the relative position of positive and negative numbers through a common application.

Solution

    a 64,868 feet

    b. Diagram should show 29,028 above a representation of sea level as 0, and 35,840 further below the representation of sea level.

Standard: Understand numbers, ways of representing numbers, relationships among numbers, and number systems

Expectation: Describe classes of numbers according to characteristics such as the nature of their factors

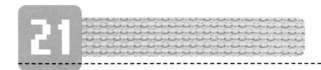

José created a game using two number cubes of different colors. The green cube had ODD multiples of 3, and the red cube had EVEN multiples of 3.

a. What was the color of the cube that had the number 6?
b. List SIX numbers that could be on the OTHER cube.
c. Could José design the same game using multiples of 4? Explain your answer.

> **Source:** Kentucky Mathematics, Form 4a, Grade 5 (sample released items 1998–1999, item 11: "Number Cubes")
>
> **About the mathematics:** Students must understand odd and even numbers, and recognize the multiples of 3 and 4.
>
> **Solution**
>   A. Red
>   B. 3, 9, 15, 21, 27, 33, 39, 45, . . .
>   C. No—multiples of 4 are all even.

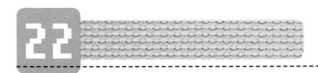

Patrick had only quarters, dimes, and nickels to buy snacks. He spent all his money and received no change. Could he have spent 99¢? Justify your answer.

> **About the mathematics:** This item requires an understanding of the results of adding multiples of 5.
>
> **Solution:** No, he needs 4 pennies. If all he has are quarters (25¢), dimes (10¢), and nickels (5¢), he can get only totals that end in 5 or 0.

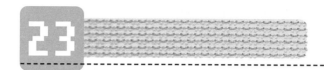

In Bob's town, even-numbered streets run north and south, and odd-numbered streets run east and west. Which is a north-and-south street?

a. 42nd Street
b. 37th Street
c. 19th Street
d. 73th Street

Source: New Standards Project
About the mathematics: This item requires students to identify an even number from a collection of four ordinal numbers.
Solution: a

Standard: Understand meanings of operations and how they relate to one another

Expectation: Understand various meanings of multiplication and division

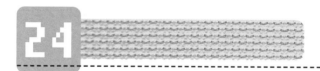

Sharon and Jessica have a bag of 156 candies. They want to find the greatest number of candies to put into 12 bags so that each bag will have the same amount.

Sharon says they should see how many times they can subtract 12 from 156.
Jessica says they should divide 156 by 12.
Who is correct? Sharon, Jessica, both, or neither?

How do you know?

About the mathematics: This item requires an understanding of two meanings of division.
Solution: Both are correct.
Teacher note: The explanation might state that division is the same as subtracting lots of times, or might demonstrate that the results are the same.

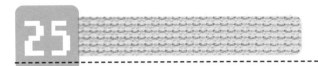

25

The teacher has 30 feet of rope. She cuts off pieces 4 feet long to make jump ropes for her class. Before she finishes, a student predicts that she will have 2 feet of rope left over.

Is the student correct? How do you know? Explain using words or a diagram.

About the mathematics: Students must understand the effect of dividing 30 into groups of 4.
Solution: The student is correct. The explanation might be a drawing, or a continuation of grouping the 30 feet into lengths of 4 feet, or an explanation of the number sentence $30 \div 4 = 7$ R2.

Standard: Understand meanings of operations and how they relate to one another

Expectation: Understand the effects of multiplying and dividing whole numbers

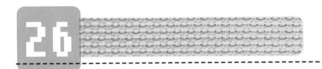

26

Which word problem below could be represented by the number sentence $6 \times 3 = 18$?

a. Steve had 6 baseball cards. He bought 3 more cards. How many cards does he now have?

b. Steve bought 6 baseball card packages with 3 cards in each package. How many cards did he buy?

c. Steve had 6 baseball cards. He gave away 3 of them. How many cards did he have left?

d. Steve had 6 baseball cards. He put the cards in 3 equal stacks. How many baseball cards were in each stack?

About the mathematics: This item requires the ability to represent a situation with a number sentence.

Solution: b

Mrs. Forest wanted to plan how to contact her students by phone in case the field trip they were going on the next day needed to be canceled. She decided to call 1 student, who would then call 2 other students. Each of these students would then call 2 other students. This telephone chain would continue until all students had been called. Mrs. Forest has 31 students. How many students will need to make phone calls if Mrs. Forest calls the first student?

How do you know? Show your work.

Source: Exemplars

About the mathematics: This item requires an understanding of the effects of repeatedly multiplying by 2.

Solution: A total of 15 students need to make phone calls.

Teacher note: The explanation could be narrative or could include a tree diagram.

Rubric: A sample rubric appears on the following page.

Rubric

Four points
- Fully meets criteria.
- Has correct answer and clear explanation supported by written work, which may include tree diagrams to illustrate the situation.

Three points
- Adequately meets criteria.
- Has correct answer and explanation, although the explanation may be more generalized or incomplete.
- The answer may be incorrect, but the error results from a computation or counting mistake rather than a flawed solution strategy.

Two points
A combination of the following flaws:
- An incorrect answer results from a flawed solution strategy but includes enough explanation that the reader can determine where the student went wrong.
- The correct answer is accompanied by some supporting written work, but the thought process is inferred by reader rather than explained by student.

One point
- The answer is correct answer, but no supporting work whatsoever is supplied.

Zero points
- No answer or incorrect answer
- Insufficient work to determine the student's thought process

28

Dylan has not learned how to multiply big numbers, but he wants to know the answer to 6517×6. He is sure there is another way to get the answer. Which plan can he follow?

a. Find $6517 + 6517$, then double the sum.
b. Find $6517 + 6517 + 6517$, then double the sum.
c. Find $(6 \times 6) + (5 \times 6) + (1 \times 6) + (7 \times 6)$
d. Find $6517 + 6517 + 6517$, then double the sum, then double that sum.

> **Teacher note:** Another way to ask the question is, Is there another way Dylan could find the answer? This wording would allow students more flexibility in solving the problem and would provide additional evidence of the student's understanding of multiplication.
> **Source:** Nova Scotia Elementary Mathematics Program Assessment (2003, item 33)
> **About the mathematics:** Students must understand the meaning of multiplying by 6.
> **Solution:** b

Standard: Understand meanings of operations and how they relate to one another

Expectation: Identify and use relationships between operations, such as division as the inverse of multiplication, to solve problems

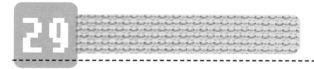

29

The sum of two numbers is 20 and their difference is 12. If you divide the larger number by the smaller number, the quotient is 4. What are the two numbers?

About the mathematics: Students must be able to use addition and subtraction to reason about number. (Note that the second clue is not necessary to solve the problem but does confirm the correct pair of numbers.)
Solution: 16 and 4

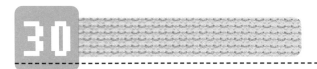

Judy is filling bags of candy for her party. She has 15 candies and 8 bags. Write a number sentence that shows how many more candies she needs so she can put 4 candies in each bag.

> **About the mathematics:** Students must understand division as equal groups and be able to work with division in a two-step process.
> **Solution:** $4 \times 8 - 15 = 17$. Judy needs 17 more candies to have 32, which would mean she could have 4 candies in each of 8 bags.

Standard: Understand meanings of operations and how they relate to one another

Expectation: Understand and use properties of operations, such as the distributivity of multiplication over addition

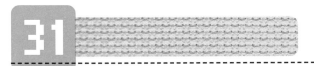

If the sum of 27 and 48 is divided by 3, is the result the same as dividing 27 by 3 and 48 by 3 and adding the two quotients? How do you know?

> **About the mathematics:** Depending on the answer to "How do you know," this item requires an understanding of the distributive property, or the ability to correctly add and divide one- and two-digit numbers.

Solution: Yes

$$(27 + 48) \div 3 = 75 \div 3 = 25$$
$$27 \div 3 = 9; \; 48 \div 3 = 16; \; 9 + 16 = 25$$

Or:

We are finding how many 3s are in 27 and then how many 3s are in 48, which is the same as finding how many 3s are in 27 + 48.

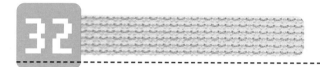

Greg had 64 baseball cards. He gave 12 cards to his sister. Then he divided the remaining cards equally among his FOUR friends. How many cards did each of his friends get?

How do you know?

Source: Adapted from the Kentucky Mathematics, Grade 5 (January 2004, sample released items, item 1)

About the mathematics: Depending on the answer to "How do you know," this item requires an understanding of the distributive property, or the ability to correctly subtract and divide one- and two-digit numbers.

Solution: $(64 - 12) \div 4 = 52 \div 4 = 13$. Each friend got 13 cards. After Greg gave 12 cards to his sister, he had 52 left. Then he gave each of his four friends the same number of cards, so they each got 13 cards.

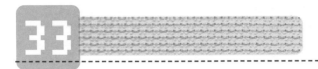

A schoolyard contains only bicycles and wagons like those in the figure above. On Monday there were 3 bicycles and 2 wagons in the schoolyard. How many wheels were in the schoolyard?

Source: National Assessment of Educational Progress (2003, block 4M7, item 5)

About the mathematics: This item involves representing a situation with a number sentence to find a solution. It can also be solved with a sketch.

Solution

3 bicycles × 2 wheels per bicycle = 6 wheels

2 wagons × 4 wheels per wagon = 8 wheels

6 wheels + 8 wheels = 14 wheels

Student Work

Correct Student Response

This student should be encouraged to label all his or her work.

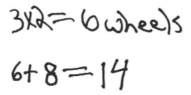

Partially Correct Student Response

This student should be encouraged to label all her or his work.

$$6 + 8 = 14$$

Incorrect Student Response

This student should be encouraged to show his or her work.

5

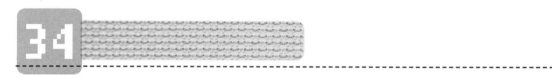

On Tuesday the total number of wheels in the schoolyard was 24. There are several ways this could happen.

a. How many bicycles and how many wagons could there be for this to happen?
   Show all your work.
   Number of bicycles _____
   Number of wagons _____

b. Find another way that this could happen. Show all your work.
   Number of bicycles _____
   Number of wagons _____

> **Source:** National Assessment of Educational Progress (2003, block 4M7, item 6)
>
> **About the mathematics:** This item involves finding multiple solutions where more than one solution is possible.
>
> **Solution:** Possible answers include 6 bicycles and 3 wagons or 8 bicycles and 2 wagons.

Standard: Compute fluently and make reasonable estimates

Expectation: Develop fluency with basic number combinations for multiplication and division and use these combinations to mentally compute related problems, such as 30×50

35

A gardener is planting a flowerbed as shown.

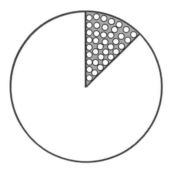

The gardener has planted 85 tulips so far. What is the BEST ESTIMATE for the total number of tulips that will be in the garden?

a. 150 to 200 tulips
b. 300 to 400 tulips
c. 650 to 750 tulips
d. 1200 to 1300 tulips

Source: Adapted from Massachusetts Comprehensive Assessment System: Grade 4, Mathematics (release of May 1999 test items, item 8)

About the mathematics: Students demonstrate an understanding of the representation of a fractional part, make a reasonable estimate of the size of the fractional piece, and from that estimate determine how many pieces would constitute the whole flowerbed. They then make a reasonable estimate of 85 times the number of pieces, and locate the result among the choices.

Solution: c. The fractional part of the circle represented appears to be 1/8, so 8 × 85 tulips will be planted in the whole flowerbed. A reasonable estimate of 8 × 85 is 8 × 100 = 800. But the number will be less than 800, since 85 is less than 100, so a reasonable answer would be c, 650–750 tulips.

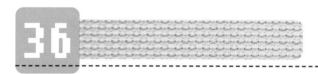

The school library is moving to a new location. The librarian has 1487 books to put into boxes. Each box can hold 15 books. *About* how many boxes will she need to use?

a. 5
b. 10
c. 100
d. 1000

About the mathematics: Students must make a reasonable estimate of the result of dividing a four-digit number by a two-digit number by realizing that 1487 is close to 1500, which is 100 times 15.

Solution: c

Standard: Compute fluently and make reasonable estimates

Expectation: Develop fluency in adding, subtracting, multiplying, and dividing whole numbers

37

A store sells 168 tapes each week. How many tapes does it sell in 24 weeks? Show all your work.

> **Source:** Adapted from National Assessment of Educational Progress (1992, block 4M12, item 3)
>
> **About the mathematics:** Students must be able to multiply a three-digit number by a two-digit number accurately.
>
> **Solution:** 4032
>
> **Teacher note:** One way to determine the result is to realize that multiplying by 24 is approximately equivalent to multiplying by 25, which is equivalent to dividing by 4 and multiplying by 100: 168 divided by 4 is 42, and 42 multiplied by 100 is 4200. To get the exact result, take 168 away from 4200 to get 4032.

38

Max bought 50 plants for his garden. He plans to put 8 plants in each row. How many complete rows of 8 plants can he make?
How do you know?

> **Source:** Adapted from National Assessment of Educational Progress (1990, block 4M7, item 16)
>
> **About the mathematics:** This item requires the ability to choose the correct operation for a context, and to divide 50 by 8 and deal with the remainder appropriately.

Solution: Six complete rows; 6 rows with 8 plants in each row will require 48 plants. Only 2 plants will be left over from the 50 plants Max bought, not enough for another complete row.

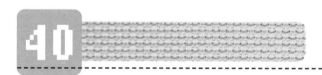

The O'Malley family collected 236 shells on a recent trip to the beach. The 4 O'Malley sisters agreed to share equally the shells collected by their family.

How many shells did each sister get? Show how you got your answer.

Source: New Standards Project, Grade 4, Mathematics (test item "Shells")
About the mathematics: Students must recognize a situation that requires division, as well as be able to divide a three-digit number by a one-digit number.
Solution: Each sister got 59 shells.

$$236 \div 4 = 59$$

Or:
I know that $240 \div 4 = 60$, but I had 4 less than 240, so I have to take one shell away from each sister: $60 - 1 = 59$.

A builder needs to purchase 21,508 bricks. The local brick supplier had only 19,689 bricks in stock.

How many bricks will the brick supplier need to order to have exactly the number that the builder needs?

Show how you got your answer.

Source: New Standards Project, Form E, Mathematics (p. 19, test item "Bricks")
About the mathematics: Students must recognize a situation that requires subtraction, as well as be able to subtract one 5-digit number from another 5-digit number.
Solution: 1,819 bricks

$$21,508 - 19,689 = 1,819$$

Or:
Use counting on:

$$19,689 + 11 = 19,700$$
$$19,700 + 300 = 20,000$$
$$20,000 + 1508 = 21,508$$
$$1,508 + 300 + 11 = 1,819$$

Standard: Compute fluently and make reasonable estimates

Expectation: Develop and use strategies to estimate the results of whole-number computations and to judge the reasonableness of such results

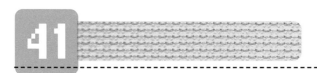

41

Mike spent $15.85 for a DVD and $3.25 on popcorn. Which is the BEST ESTIMATE of the amount of money he spent?

a. About $190
b. About $18
c. About $19
d. About $20

About the mathematics: Given the choice of answers, students are asked to choose the best estimate from among rounding up, rounding down, and rounding to the nearest whole-dollar amount.
Solution: c

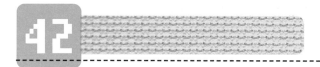

Steve bought 7 bags of peaches that each cost $2.98. He also bought juice for $7.65. What can you say about what he spent altogether?

a. He spent almost $30.00.
b. He spent almost $15.00.
c. He spent less than $21.00.
d. He spent less than $12.00.

About the mathematics: Students must recognize a situation that requires multiplication and addition, make a reasonable estimate of the cost of 7 bags of peaches at $2.98, then add the result to $7.65. They then choose the item that most closely describes the result.

Solution: a

Standard: Compute fluently and make reasonable estimates

Expectation: Develop and use strategies to estimate computations involving fractions and decimals in situations relevant to students' experience

If $1\frac{1}{3}$ cups of flour are needed for a batch of cookies, how many cups of flour will be needed for 3 batches?

How do you know?

Source: Adapted from the National Assessment of Educational Progress (1992, block 4M7, item 6)

About the mathematics: Students must be able to compute with simple fractions.

Solution: 4 cups of flour

1 $\frac{1}{3}$ cups of flour per batch of cookies $\times$ 3 batches of cookies = 4 cups of flour.

Or:

For 3 batches I need 3 full cups (1 cup per batch for 3 batches) and another 3 one-third cups, which make another full cup. Add 3 cups and 1 cup to get 4 cups.

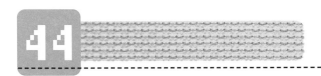

Chen bought one model plane, one tube of glue, and one can of paint.

The cost of each item is shown in the figure above. There was no sales tax. How much change should he have received from $10.00?

How do you know?

Source: Adapted from National Assessment of Educational Progress (1990, block 4M9, item 7)

About the mathematics: This item involves calculating cost of several items, then determining how much change should be given.

Solution: $10.00 – ($4.99 + $1.29 + $2.19) = $1.53.

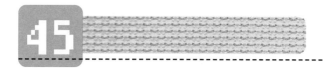

At a class party, 3 pizzas were ordered for the children. Each pizza was divided into 8 equal slices. Each child ate 2 slices, and there was a quarter of one pizza left. How many children were at the party?

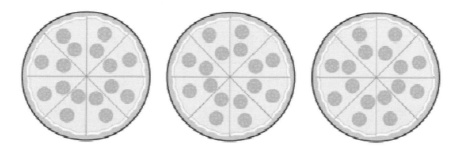

How do you know?

Source: Adapted from the Massachusetts Comprehensive Assessment System: Grade 4, Mathematics (release of spring 2002 test items, item 20)

About the mathematics: Students must demonstrate an understanding of equal groups and of simple fractions.

Solution: 11

Explanation: There were 3 pizzas with 8 pieces each, so there were 24 pieces ($3 \times 8 = 24$). A quarter of one pizza was left. Since each pizza was divided into 8 pieces, 2 pieces were left (one quarter of 8 is 2). So only 22 pieces were eaten ($24 - 2 = 22$). Each child ate 2 slices, so there were 11 children at the party ($22 \div 2 = 11$).

46

Jesse was riding with his mom on the highway. They passed this sign:

> **Davis St. Exit** $1\frac{3}{4}$ **miles**
>
> **Marina Blvd. Exit** $2\frac{1}{4}$ **miles**

Jesse and his mom kept driving. A couple of minutes later, Jesse saw a second sign:

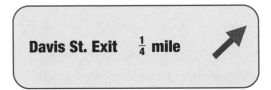

> **Davis St. Exit** $\frac{1}{4}$ **mile**   ↗

How far were Jesse and his mom from the Marina Blvd. exit?

Show or describe how you know.

> **Source:** Adapted from Balanced Assessment, Elementary Grades, Package 1 (task 9: "Highway Signs")
>
> **About the mathematics:** This item requires students to compute with simple fractions.
>
> **Solution:** The first sign they saw said the Davis Street exit was $1\frac{3}{4}$ miles away. The next sign said the same exit was $\frac{1}{4}$ mile away. The distance they traveled was $1\frac{3}{4} - \frac{1}{4}$, or $1\frac{1}{2}$, miles. The first sign said the Marina Boulevard exit was $2\frac{1}{4}$ miles away, and they had traveled $1\frac{1}{2}$ miles, so they were $\frac{3}{4}$ miles from the Marina Boulevard exit.

Standard: Compute fluently and make reasonable estimates

Expectation: Use visual models, benchmarks, and equivalent forms to add and subtract commonly used fractions and decimals.

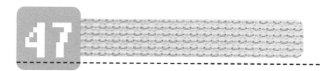

Use the picture of marbles below to answer the question.

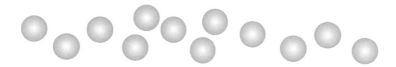

There were 12 marbles on the floor. Lisa picked up $\frac{1}{2}$ of the 12 marbles, and Tom picked up $\frac{1}{4}$ of the 12 marbles.

a. How many marbles were picked up?
b. What fraction of the 12 marbles was picked up?

How do you know?

> **Source:** Adapted from the Massachusetts Comprehensive Assessment System, Grade 4, Mathematics (release of spring 2000 test items)
> **About the mathematics:** To solve this item, students must be able to find $\frac{1}{2}$ and $\frac{1}{4}$ of 12.
> **Solution**
>   a. 9 marbles
>   b. $\frac{9}{12}$, or $\frac{3}{4}$, of the 12 marbles
> **Explanation:** Lisa picked up half of 12, which is 6 marbles. Tom picked up $\frac{1}{4}$ of 12, which is 3 marbles. Add the two quantities: $6 + 3 = 9$. Either 9 out of 12 is equivalent to 3 out of 4, or $\frac{1}{2} + \frac{1}{4} = \frac{3}{4}$.

48

Amy, Elizabeth, Katie, Gretchen, and Deb love chocolate. One afternoon they each had a large chocolate bar. Each chocolate bar was the same size. Here is what each girl ate:

Amy:	two-sixths of her chocolate bar
Elizabeth:	two-thirds of her chocolate bar
Katie:	three-fourths of her chocolate bar
Gretchen:	one-half of her chocolate bar
Deb:	one-third of her chocolate bar

Who ate the most chocolate?
Who ate the least chocolate?
How much chocolate did they eat altogether?

Explain your answers in words, numbers, and diagrams.

Source: Adapted from Exemplars, Vol. 7, Mathematics (winter 2000, "Lots and Lots of Chocolate" item)

About the mathematics: To be successful, students must understand relative size of fractions and be able to combine fractions.

Solution

Katie ate the most chocolate.

Amy and Deb at the least chocolate.

Altogether they ate $2\,^7/_{12}$ chocolate bars.

Katie ate the most, because $^3/_4$ is larger than all the other fractions.

Amy and Deb at the same amount, because $^2/_6$ is equivalent to $^1/_3$, and both are smaller than all the other fractions.

If you make fractions equivalent to the amount each girl ate by using a denominator of 12, you get the following:

Amy: $^4/_{12}$ of her chocolate bar

Elizabeth: $^8/_{12}$ of her chocolate bar

Katie: $^9/_{12}$ of her chocolate bar

Gretchen: $^6/_{12}$ of her chocolate bar

Deb: $^4/_{12}$ of her chocolate bar

In order from largest to smallest, the fractions are $^3/_4 > ^2/_3 > ^1/_2 > ^1/_3$.

$$^2/_6 + {}^2/_3 + {}^3/_4 + {}^1/_2 + {}^1/_3 = {}^4/_{12} + {}^8/_{12} + {}^9/_{12} + {}^6/_{12} + {}^4/_{12}$$

$$= {}^{31}/_{12}, \text{ or } 2\,{}^7/_{12}$$

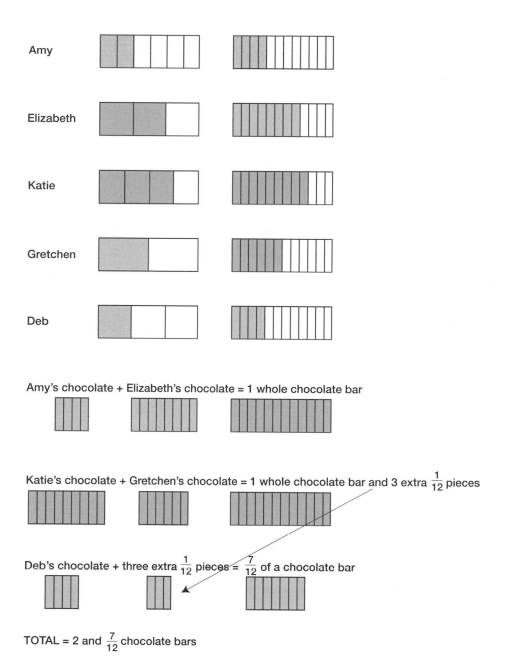

Amy

Elizabeth

Katie

Gretchen

Deb

Amy's chocolate + Elizabeth's chocolate = 1 whole chocolate bar

Katie's chocolate + Gretchen's chocolate = 1 whole chocolate bar and 3 extra $\frac{1}{12}$ pieces

Deb's chocolate + three extra $\frac{1}{12}$ pieces = $\frac{7}{12}$ of a chocolate bar

TOTAL = 2 and $\frac{7}{12}$ chocolate bars

Standard: Compute fluently and make reasonable estimates

Expectation: Select appropriate methods and tools for computing with whole numbers from among mental computation, estimation, calculators, and paper and pencil according to the context and nature of the computation and use the selected method or tool

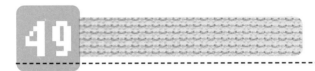

49

The length of a dinosaur was reported to have been 80 feet (rounded to the nearest 10 feet). What length other than 80 feet could have been the actual length of this dinosaur?

How do you know?

> **Source:** Adapted from National Assessment of Educational Progress (1992, block 4M1 5, item 9)
> **About the mathematics:** This item requires an understanding of the results of rounding to the nearest 10.
> **Solution:** Any answer between 75 feet and just under 85 feet is acceptable.

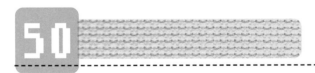

50

What is the quickest way to solve the problem 12×25?

a. Mental computation
b. Estimation
c. Paper and pencil
d. Calculator

Why? Explain your thinking.

Teacher note: The student work we obtained was very interesting, and we have included student work for each of the choices in the chapter on professional development. The calculator was by far the most popular choice, and this outcome might happen in your classroom, too. The result can lead to a discussion about using number sense and parameters for choosing a calculator as the more appropriate tool.

About the mathematics: This item requires the ability to multiply a two-digit number by a two-digit number correctly. This problem could be done most efficiently with mental computation, but students can make convincing arguments for other methods.

Solution: Answers may vary; only choice b (estimation) is incorrect, because the student was asked to "solve," not to estimate.

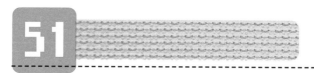

Rose is 4 years older than Natalie. Natalie is 5 years older than Emma. Together the three sisters' ages equal 26. How old is each girl?

Show and explain exactly how you figured it out.

Source: Balanced Assessment, Elementary Grades, Package 1 (task 14: "Sisters")

About the mathematics: This item requires the ability to represent and analyze a mathematical situation. Students must determine a strategy that will enable them to make comparisons among the ages of the three sisters.

Solution: Emma is 4, Natalie is 9, and Rose is 13. The ages sum to 4 + 9 + 13 = 26.

One possible explanation would involve making a chart, such as the one below.

Emma	Natalie	Rose	Total Ages
1	6	10	17
2	7	11	20
3	8	12	23
4	9	13	26
5	10	14	29
6	11	15	32

Algebra

THE FOCUS of algebra is on patterns, relations, and functions and the ability to analyze situations using a variety of representations. Algebra provides a foundation for complex and divergent thinking. Students use algebra to model and understand quantitative relationships in the real world.

> In grades 3–5 students should investigate numerical and geometric patterns and express them mathematically in words or symbols. They should analyze the structure of the pattern and how it grows or changes, organize this information systematically, and use their analysis to develop generalizations abut the mathematical relationships in the pattern.[1] … Students should be encouraged to explain these patterns verbally and to make predictions about what will happen if the sequence is continued.[2]

As students develop algebraic reasoning, they become more proficient in analyzing relationships, identifying the similarities and differences between various functions, and form generalizations about geometric and numerical patterns. "Students need to feel comfortable using various techniques for organizing and expressing ideas about relationships and functions."[3]

In assessing a student's algebraic thinking, we must determine the student's ability to move among various representations, explain relationships, and judge the reasonableness of solutions.

---

1 National Council of Teachers of Mathematics (2000, p. 149)
2 National Council of Teachers of Mathematics (2000, p. 194)
3 National Council of Teachers of Mathematics (2000, p. 206)

Algebra Assessment Items

Standard: Understand patterns, relations and functions

Expectation: Describe, extend, and make generalizations about geometric and numeric patterns

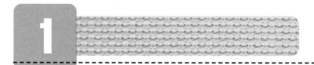

Teacher note: Students should have multiple opportunities to investigate patterns, to find a missing number or object, or to extend the pattern. Several different types of patterns are presented here. Any one of these could be adapted to meet your students' needs. In addition, the multiple-choice items can easily be changed to short-response or even extended-response items with the request for a picture or words to explain the answer.

A city bus stops in front of your home. The following sequence shows the different times the bus will stop.

8:14 A.M.   8:26 A.M.   8:38 A.M.

Find the next two times the bus will stop if it continues according to the pattern above.

About the mathematics: This item involves extending a time pattern.
Solution: 8:50 A.M., 9:02 A.M.

2

Given:

Which of the following numeric patterns best represents the geometric pattern above?

a. 1, 3, 9, 12
b. 1, 2, 4, 8
c. 1, 3, 6, 9
d. 1, 3, 6, 10

> **About the mathematics:** The solution involves matching a geometric pattern with an associated numerical pattern.
> **Solution:** d

3

If this pattern continues, what will the eleventh shape look like?

$$\Leftarrow, \Uparrow, \Rightarrow, \Downarrow, \Leftarrow, \Uparrow, \Rightarrow, \Downarrow, \Leftarrow,$$

> **About the mathematics:** This item involves identifying and extending a geometric pattern.
> **Solution:** $\Rightarrow$

Find the missing number in each of the patterns below.

A. 2, 5, 11, 23, _____, 95, 191
B. 1, 2, 5, 10, 17, _____, 37

> **About the mathematics:** This item involves identifying a nonlinear growth pattern.
> **Solution:** A's missing number is 47, and B's missing number is 26.

Fill in the missing numbers for the pattern below.

25, 20, _____, _____, 19, 14, 16, 11, 13, 8

> **About the mathematics:** The solution involves identifying a pattern in which the change between terms is alternating.
> **Solution:** 22, 17

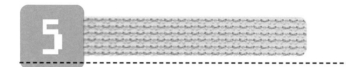

A pattern was used to determine the number of black tiles and the number of white tiles in each figure below.

Figure 1   Figure 2   Figure 3

If the pattern continues, how many black tiles will be in figure 5? How do you know?

Source: Adapted from Massachusetts Comprehensive Assessment System, Mathematics, Grade 4 (release items 2002, item 26)

About the mathematics: For this item, students identify a geometric pattern and the numerical pattern associated with it.

Solution: Five; justifications will vary but may include an explanation and a sketch like the following:

Figure 4 will have black triangles on either end of the figure, as illustrated above, for a total of five black triangles. In figure 5, the pattern will have white tiles added at either end, but this addition will not change the total number of black tiles, so figure 5 will still contain five black tiles.

7

A rule was used to make the pattern of figures shown below.

a. Draw the next 5 figures in the pattern. Describe the rule used to make the pattern.
b. Draw the 100th figure in the pattern. Explain how you know what the figure should look like.

Source: Massachusetts Comprehensive Assessment System, Mathematics, Grade 4 (release items 2003, item 13)

About the mathematics: Part a extends the pattern; part b requires recognizing the pattern, since drawing 100 figures is not practical.

Solution

a.

b. Every fourth figure looks like the one below, and since 100 is a multiple of 4, it will also look like this one.

Standard: Understand patterns, relations, and functions

Expectation: Represent and analyze patterns and functions, using words, tables and graphs

---

The table shows the cost of hamburgers.

If the pattern continues, what will be the cost for 6 hamburgers?

a. $12.50
b. $13.50
c. $13.75
d. $14.25

Number of Hamburgers	Total Cost
1	$ 2.25
2	$ 4.50
3	$ 6.75
4	$ 9.00
5	$11.25

Source: Commonwealth of Virginia/Department of Education, Grade 5 (2001, p. 80, item 43)

About the mathematics: The solution involves identifying and extending a numerical pattern.

Solution: b

9

The table shows how much money Harold's Produce Store can make by selling boxes of fruit.

Number of Boxes Sold	Money Made
1	$4
3	$12
5	$20
7	$28
9	
10	

If the pattern in the table continues, how much money can the store make by selling 9 boxes? _____ By selling 10 boxes? _____

Source: Adapted from Commonwealth of Virginia/Department of Education, Grade 3 (2000, p. 55, item 48)

About the mathematics: For this item, students identify and extend a numerical pattern in which the terms (in this instance, the number of boxes sold) are not consecutive.

Solution: $36; $40

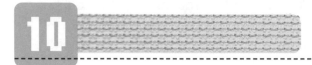

10

The table shows the time each bus leaves the station in the morning. If the pattern continues, what time should bus 7 leave the station? _____

Bus	Time
1	8:30
2	8:45
3	9:00
4	9:15
5	9:30
6	9:45
7	
8	
9	

If John wants to take the bus at 10:30, which bus should he take? _____

Source: Adapted from Commonwealth of Virginia/Department of Education, Grade 3 (2001, p. 55, item 47)

About the mathematics: This item involves extending a time pattern and associating the pattern with a numerical sequence (in this instance, bus numbers).

Solution: 10:00; bus 9

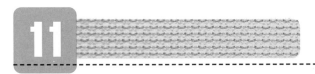

11

Children's pictures are to be hung in a line as shown in the following figure. Pictures that are hung next to each other share a tack.

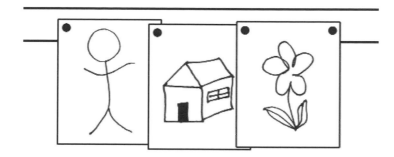

How many tacks are needed to hang 28 pictures in this way?

How do you know?

Source: Adapted from National Assessment of Educational Progress (1992, block 4M7, item 08)
About the mathematics: The solution requires identifying a pattern and extending it.
Solution: 29

12

Look at the following trapezoids, and complete the table.

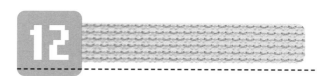

A. If you had 50 trapezoids, how many sides would you have? Explain how you know.
B. Write an equation that would help you find the number of sides for any number of trapezoids.

# of trapezoids	# of sides
1	4
2	8
3	12
4	
5	
6	
7	
8	
9	
10	

Source: Adapted from *Connect to NCTM Standards 2000* (Creative Publications 2000)

About the mathematics: This item requires students to identify and abstract a numerical pattern associated with a geometric pattern.

Solution

   A. 50 trapezoids will have 200 sides because each trapezoid will have 4 sides.

   B. $s = t \times 4$, where s is the number of sides and t is the number of trapezoids.

Standard: Represent and analyze mathematical situations and structures using algebraic symbols

Expectation: Identify such properties as commutativity, associativity, and distributivity and use them to compute with whole numbers

13

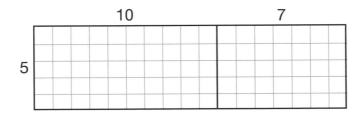

10   7

5

Given the rectangular array above, complete the equation to describe the area of the array.

_____ + _____ = 85

About the mathematics: The solution involves using the distributive property to find the area of an array.
Solution: 50 + 35, or (5 × 10) + (5 × 7)

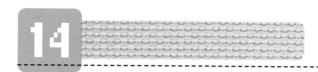

Jay shot 4 arrows at the target. His total score was 45. Which of these scores is not a possible result of Jay's 4 shots.

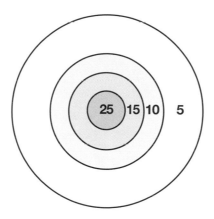

a. $25 + (2 \times 5) + 10$
b. $15 + (3 \times 10)$
c. $(2 \times 15) + 10 + 5$
d. $25 + 5 + (2 \times 10)$

Source: *Comprehensive Assessment of Mathematic Strategies* (Curriculum Associates, 2000)
About the mathematics: To solve this item, students employ the order of operations in computing number strings.
Solution: d

15

The difference between 85 and 53 is 32. Meredith added some number to 85 and then added the same number to 53. What would be the difference between the two new numbers?

a. More than 32
b. Less than 32
c. 32
d. It depends on the number added to 85 and 53.

How do you know?

Source: Adapted from National Assessment of Educational Progress (1990, block 4M9, item11)

About the mathematics: Students must understand that the difference between two numbers is preserved when equal amounts are added to the two numbers.

Solution: c. Explanations will vary; imagery of a number line is useful.

Standard: Represent and analyze mathematical situations and structures using algebraic symbols

Expectation: Represent the idea of a variable as an unknown quantity using a letter or a symbol

16

The following values are assigned to variables M, K and L:

$$M = 2 \qquad K = 6 \qquad L = 3$$

Find the value of $K + L - M$.

a. 1
b. 5
c. 7
d. 11

Source: National Assessment of Educational Progress (2003, block 4M10, item 08)
About the mathematics: This item involves substituting numbers into an algebraic expression.
Solution: c

The two number sentences shown below are true.

$$\square + \square = 6$$

$$\triangle + \square = 12$$

What values for $\triangle$ and $\square$ will make both number sentences true? Justify your answer.

About the mathematics: The solution requires solving for unknowns.
Solution: $\triangle$ represents 9, and $\square$ represents 3.

18

The two number sentences shown below are true.

$$\square - \bigcirc = 6$$

$$\bigcirc + \bigcirc = 2$$

If both equations shown above are true, which of the following equations must also be true?

a. $\square \times \bigcirc = \square$

b. $\bigcirc \times 2 = \bigcirc$

c. $\square + \square = 12$

d. $\square + \bigcirc = \square$

Source: Massachusetts Comprehensive Assessment System, Mathematics, Grade 4 (release of spring 2003 test items, item 6)
About the mathematics: This item involves solving for unknowns.
Solution: a

19

Each shape stands for a different number. All shapes that are the same stand for the same answer. Find the number for the square.

$$\square + \triangle = 35 \qquad \square + \bigcirc = 27$$

$$\bigcirc + \triangle = 18 \qquad \square = \,?$$

Source: Greenes, Findell, Gavin, and Sheffield, *Awesome Math Problems for Creative Thinking, Grade 5* (Chicago: Creative Publications, 2000, p. 45)
About the mathematics: Students solve systems of equations by using given information to solve for unknowns.
Solution: 22

Standard: Represent and analyze mathematical situations and structures using algebraic symbols

Expectation: Express mathematical relationships using equations

Micah left for school with 4 boxes of pencils. Each box had 6 pencils. At school, he gave away 4 pencils from one box. Which number sentence below can be used to find the total number of pencils that were left?

a. $4 \times 6 - 4 = \square$
b. $4 \times 6 + 2 = \square$
c. $3 \times 6 + 4 = \square$
d. $3 \times 6 - 2 = \square$

Source: Massachusetts Comprehensive Assessment System, Mathematics, Grade 4 (release of spring 2002 test items, item 18)
About the mathematics: The solution involves matching the structure of a problem with the number sentence that represents the solution.
Solution: a

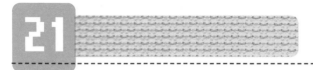

When numbers are put into an input-output machine, the following results occur. Find the rule that was used to change the numbers in the input column to the numbers in the output column.

Input A	Output B
3	6
5	10
6	12

Write an equation to represent your rule.

> **About the mathematics:** This item involves finding a rule and writing an equation to represent that rule.
>
> **Solution:** The rule is to multiply the number in the input column by 2 to get the number in the output column. Equation: Input × 2 = Output, or A × 2 = B.
>
> **Teacher note:** Students should have multiple opportunities to solve similar problems in which the number in the input column is increased or decreased by a constant value. They should also have opportunities to work with input-output tables that contain missing values in both the input and the output columns. Students should be encouraged to explain what is happening, in words as well as with mathematical notation.

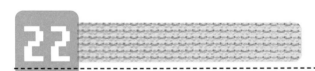

It costs 20¢ to mail a postcard and 37¢ to mail a letter.

Stamps	
Postcard	20¢
Letter	37¢

a. Roxie sent 10 postcards to her relatives and some letters to her friends. She spent $5.70 on stamps to mail the postcards and letters. How many letters did she send to friends? Use pictures, numbers, or words to show or explain your answer.

b. Nick sent mail to his friends.
- He sent Tony 1 letter and 2 postcards.
- He sent Ken 2 postcards.
- He sent Owen 3 letters.

Write a number sentence to show how much money Nick spent for stamps. Be sure to include the answer in your number sentence.

> **About the mathematics:** This item requires students to write number sentences to describe mathematical relationships. Depending on how this problem is solved, in can be used to assess students' understanding of order of operations.
>
> **Solution:** a. 10 letters; b. $(0.37 + 2 \times 0.20) + (2 \times 0.20) + (3 \times 0.37) = 2.28$. The answer is $2.28, or $(37 + 2 \times 20) + (2 \times 20) + (3 \times 37) = 228$ cents.

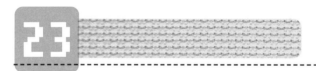

Which of these problems could be solved by using the open sentence

$$A - 5 = ?$$

a. Janis is 5 years older than Seth. If A is Seth's age, how old is Janis?
b. Todd is 5 years younger than Amelia. If A is Amelia's age in years, how old is Todd?
c. Isaac is 5 times as old as Bert. If A is Bert's age in years, how old is Isaac?
d. Nathan is one-fifth as old as Leslie. If A is Nathan's age, how old is Leslie?

> **Source:** Adapted from Commonwealth of Virginia/Department of Education Grade 5 (2001, p. 83, item 50)
>
> **About the mathematics:** The solution involves abstracting the structure of a problem to capture relationships in the problem with equations.
>
> **Solution:** b

> **Standard:** Use mathematical models to represent and understand quantitative relationships

> **Expectation:** Model problem situations with objects and use representations such as graphs, tables, and equations to draw conclusions

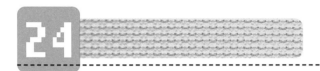

Darin is setting up for a family picnic. For seating, he placed three picnic tables end to end on the patio. The first two tables were the same length. The third table was 1 foot longer. The total length of the three tables is 25 feet.

A) Draw a diagram, and label the length of each table on the diagram to illustrate how the tables were set up.
B) What is the length of each of the shorter tables?

About the mathematics: This item involves using a mathematical model to describe a situation.

Solution

   A)

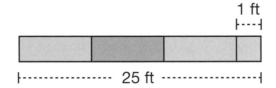

   B) The shorter tables are each 8 feet long.

25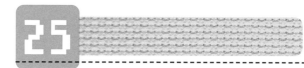

Annabelle is paid $5.00 an hour for baby-sitting for Mrs. Smith. On Friday, she baby-sits for 3 hours. Mrs. Smith calls her on Saturday to baby-sit for 3 hours. She pays her an additional 75 cents per hour on Saturday.

How much money will she make on Saturday compared with Friday? Show your work, and explain your reasoning.

About the mathematics: The solution requires developing mathematical models and comparing them to make a conclusion.
Solution: She will make 3 × 75 cents more on Saturday, or $2.25 more.

26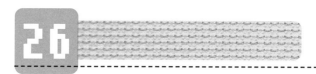

The 10 apples below weigh the same as 2 melons.

How many melons would weigh the same as 25 apples? How do you know?

Source: Adapted from Massachusetts Comprehensive Assessment System, Grade 4, Mathematics (release of spring 2003 test items, item 29)
About the mathematics: The solution requires thinking about the how the objects on the scale would relate if broken into different amounts; for example, the observation that 1 melon would balance with 5 apples is helpful in determining the balance with 25 apples.
Solution: 5 melons

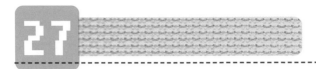

The table below shows how the chirping of a cricket is related to the temperature outside. For example, a cricket chirps 144 times each minute when the temperature is 76°.

Number of Chirps per Minute	Temperature
144	76°
152	78°
160	80°
168	82°
176	84°

What would be the number of chirps per minute when the temperature outside is 90° if this pattern stays the same?

Answer: _____

Explain how you figured out your answer.

> **Source:** National Assessment of Educational Progress (2003, block 4M7, item 20)
> **About the mathematics:** This item requires students to extend the pattern in the table.
> **Solution:** 200

Student Work

Correct Student Response

Answers: 200 chirps

Explain how you figured out your answer:

Well each 2° it goes 8 more chirps 86°it would be 184 chirps 88° it would be 192 chirps 90° it would be 200 chirps.

Satisfactory Student Response

Answers: 200

Explain how you figured out your answer:

I got my answer by contine-ing the graph until I got to 90° then I did the same on the other side

If you need more room for your work, use the space below.

Partially Correct Student Response

Answers: 194

Explain how you figured out your answer:

I went up 8 chirps each 2°

Minimal Student Response

Answers: 180

Explain how you figured out your answer:

you just figure the numbers and it will work you just add them together

Incorrect Student Response

Answers: 2

Explain how you figured out your answer:

They are counting backwards and forwards from 2.

Standard: Analyze change in various contexts

Expectation: Investigate how a change in one variable relates to a change in a second variable

28

Sheila has $20. She will receive an additional $5 an hour for doing a project for her dad. Which graph shows the relationship between the number of hours Sheila works and the total amount of money she will have?

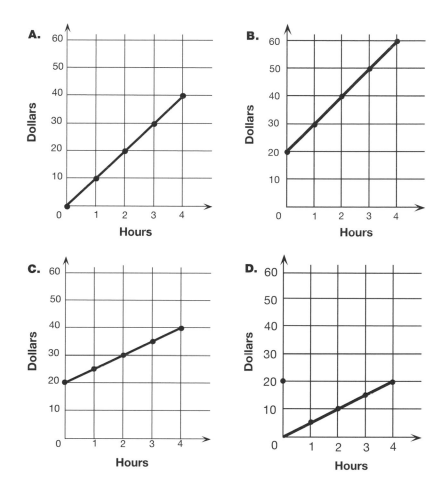

Source: Nova Scotia Elementary Mathematics Program Assessment (May 2003, item 19)

About the mathematics: This item requires ability to read a graph and connect the information with the context given.

Solution: C

29

Mary and Bill participated in a marathon to raise money. Mary had already run 2 kilometers when Bill started running, but Bill runs faster than Mary. The graph below shows the distance and time traveled by the two runners.

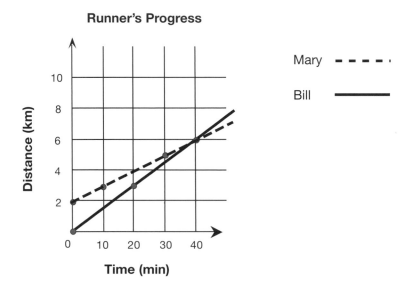

How far will each runner have traveled when Bill catches up to Mary? How do you know?

Source: Adapted Nova Scotia Elementary Mathematics Program Assessment (2003, item 14)
About the mathematics: Students are required to interpret a point of inter-section on a graph.
Solution: Both will have run 6 kilometers.

30

The following table shows how much money Jack had in his savings account for each of the past four weeks.

Week	1	2	3	4
Amount in savings	$2	$4	$6	$8

Write a number sentence that tells how much he will have in week 8 if he continues to save the same amount each week.

> **About the mathematics:** This item involves extending a pattern or identifying a function to describe the relationship between the week and amount in savings.
> **Solution:** 8 × $2 = $16.

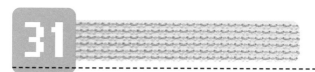

Mr. Cooper is ordering some books from a catalog. The total cost includes the cost of the book plus an additional charge for shipping. The table below shows how the total cost changes as the number of books ordered increases.

Book Costs

Number Ordered	Total Cost
1	$10.50
2	$18.50
3	$26.50
4	$34.50
5	$42.50

On the basis of the pattern shown in the table, which of the following rules could Mr. Cooper use to determine the total cost for any number of books?

a. Multiply the number of books by $9.25
b. Multiply the number of books by $10.50
c. Multiply the number of books by $10, and add $0.50 for shipping
d. Multiply the number of books by $8, and add $2.50 for shipping

Justify your answer.

Source: Adapted from Virginia Standards of Learning Assessments, Grade 5, Mathematics (spring 2003 released test, item 45)
About the mathematics: The solution involves determining a rule in a linear but nonproportional context (i.e., the *y*-intercept of the function is not zero).
Solution: d

32

A gardener plants tomatoes in a square pattern. To protect the tomatoes from insects, she surrounds the tomatoes with marigolds.

The diagram below shows the pattern of tomato plants and marigolds for any number (*n*) of rows of tomato plants.

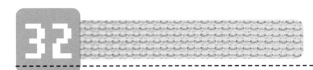 = tomato plant   ✕ = marigolds

a. Complete the table:

Rows of Tomato Plants	Number of Tomato Plants	Number of Marigolds
1		
2		
3		
4		
7		
n		

b. If the pattern continues, how many *tomato* plants will there be when *n* = 10? When *n* = 20? When there are *n* rows of tomato plants?

c. If the pattern continues, how many *marigolds* will there be when *n* = 10? When *n* = 20? When there are *n* rows of tomato plants? Describe how you know.

About the mathematics: The solution requires identifying the number of plants as related to *n*, since drawing the pattern out to the 20th figure is not practical.

Solution

a.

Rows of Tomato Plants	Number of Tomato Plants	Number of Marigolds
1	1	8
2	4	16
3	9	24
4	16	32
7	49	56
n		

b. 100 tomato plants; 400; n^2

c. 80 marigold plants; 160; $4 \times 2n$ (or other equivalent expressions, e.g., $8n$)

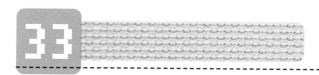

Write a number sentence to explain the rule for the following table.

Input (*n*)	Output
4	10
7	19
8	22
11	31
	43

About the mathematics: This item requires students to identify a general rule to describe the input-output boxes.

Solution: (Input times 3) minus 2 gives the output. This relationship can be expressed as $3n - 2 = $ output.

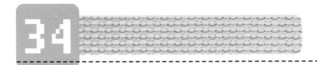

The objects on the scale shown make it balance exactly. According to this scale, if △ balances ○○○, then □ balances which of the following?

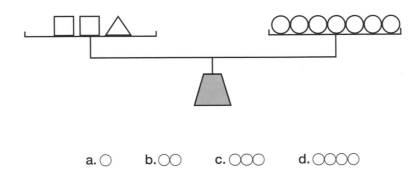

a. ○   b. ○○   c. ○○○   d. ○○○○

Source: Adapted from National Assessment of Educational Progress (2003, block 4M6, item13)

About the mathematics: The solution requires using given information to determine equivalence relationships.

Solution: b

Standard: Analyze change in various contexts

Expectation: Identify and describe situations with constant or varying rates of change and compare them

35

A rule is used to determine the number of blocks in each level of the figure below. The table shows the number of blocks that are in each level of the figure.

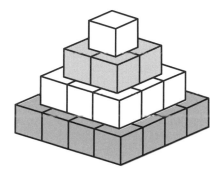

Blocks Needed

Level	Number of Blocks
1	1
2	4
3	9
4	16

How many blocks will be needed to make level 10?

How do you know?

Write a rule to show how many blocks are in level n.

> **About the mathematics:** Students identify a change in number of blocks as a function of level and make a generalization.
> **Solution:** Level 10 will have 100 blocks. The number of blocks in level n is n^2.

Geometry

THE STUDY of geometry is rich and complex. We begin to appreciate just how much can be studied through geometry by looking at the meaning of the prefix *geo-*, meaning earth, and the word *metron*, meaning measure. "The study of geometry in grades 3–5 requires thinking *and* doing. As students sort, build, draw, model, trace, measure, and construct, their capacity to visualize geometric relationships will develop."[1]

Children are engaged at an early age in the study of geometry. When building with blocks, they discover how two-dimensional shapes tile a plane and how three-dimensional forms fill up space, how they stack, and how they fit together. As children work with blocks of various kinds, they examine and analyze them and become more and more discriminating. They learn to identify and sort by knowing attributes of shapes.

"Students in grades 3–5 should consider three important kinds of transformation: reflections, translations, and rotations. They should develop greater precision as they describe the motions needed to show congruence."[2]

Students need to realize that the name of a geometric figure does not name but actually defines that figure. If children learn the name of a shape without understanding what attributes define that shape, they can end up with misconceptions. They learn to identify and sort by knowing and understanding attributes of shapes.

Meaningful experiences in geometry contribute to success in mathematics. These experiences require good instructional practices to develop concepts and language. Thoughtful assessment adapts and improves these instructional practices, thereby motivating students to learn.

---

1 National Council of Teachers of Mathematics (2000, p. 165)
2 National Council of Teachers of Mathematics (2000, p. 167)

Geometry Assessment Items

Standard: Analyze characteristics and properties of two- and three-dimensional geometric shapes and develop mathematical arguments about geometric relationships

Expectation: Identify, compare, and analyze attributes of two- and three-dimensional shapes and develop vocabulary to describe the attributes

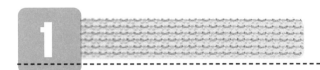

Which of the following letters has two parallel line segments?

$$\text{A} \qquad \text{T} \qquad \text{K} \qquad \text{N}$$

(A)   (B)   (C)   (D)

Source: Adapted from National Assessment of Educational Progress (1992, block 4M12, item 06)
About the mathematics: This item involves identifying attributes of a two-dimensional object.
Solution: D

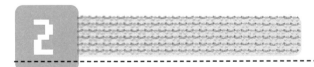

Using your ruler, draw a polygon that satisfies these two conditions.

(i)   The polygon has only two right angles.
(ii) The polygon has two congruent sides.
(iii) Label the right angles and the two congruent sides.

About the mathematics: The solution requires representing a two-dimensional shape with given characteristics.

Solution: Answers will vary. Some sample shapes include the following:

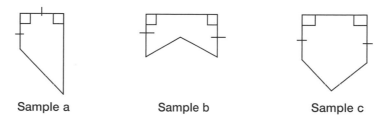

Sample a   Sample b   Sample c

Teacher note: Questions 2 and 3 ask students to identify shapes from the characteristics or attributes of those shapes. Students should have many opportunities to examine the characteristics and attributes of different shapes using models of those shapes.

Student Work

Correct Student Responses

Student has correctly drawn two congruent sides and only two right angles, and has correctly identified them.

Response 1   Response 2

Partially Correct Student Responses

Response 1
Student has correctly drawn two congruent sides and correctly identified them.

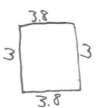

Response 2
Student has correctly drawn two right angles and
correctly identified them.

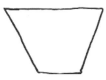

Incorrect Student Response

None of the conditions are satisfied.

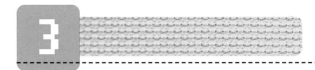

Alan says that if a figure has four sides, it must be a rectangle. Gina does not agree.
Draw a figure that shows that Gina is correct.

Source: Adapted from National Assessment of Educational Progress (2003,
block 4M6, item 07)

About the mathematics: The solution involves identifying the many two-
dimensional shapes that may share a given characteristic.

Solution: Some possible drawings include the following:

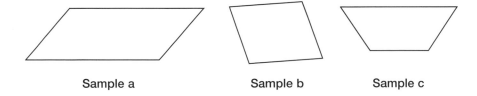

Sample a   Sample b   Sample c

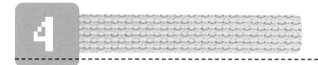

Use the trapezoid, the triangle, and the blue rhombus from your pattern blocks to complete parts A, B, and C of this question.

A. Using all three blocks, create a parallelogram. Trace your parallelogram in the space provided below.
B. Using all three blocks, create a concave polygon. Trace your concave polygon in the space provided below.
C. Using all three blocks, create a pentagon. Trace your pentagon in the space provided below.
D. Using any pattern blocks you wish, create a polygon so that all these conditions are satisfied:
   (i) The number of yellow blocks used is one-half the number of red blocks.
   (ii) The final shape has only one line of reflective symmetry, and 8 blocks in total must be used.

Source: Nova Scotia Elementary Mathematics Program Assessment (2003)
About the mathematics: This item involves creating two-dimensional shapes with given characteristics.
Solution: Solutions will vary. The following are some sample drawings:

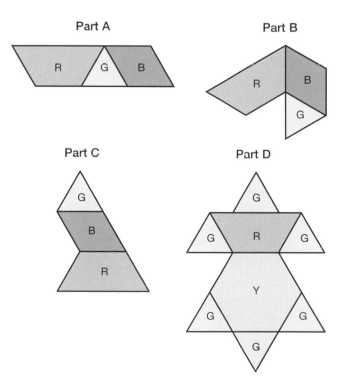

Student Work

Correct Student Response

The student correctly used all three pattern blocks to create a parallelogram.

Part A

Incorrect Student Response

The student has not used all three pattern blocks; the shape is not a parallelogram.

Part A

Correct Student Response

The student used all three pattern blocks to create a concave polygon.

Part B

Incorrect Student Response

The student used all three pattern blocks, but the shape is not a concave polygon.

Part B

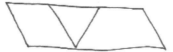

Correct Student Response

The student used all three pattern blocks to create a pentagon.

Part C

Incorrect Student Response

The student used all three pattern blocks, but the shape is not a pentagon.

Part C

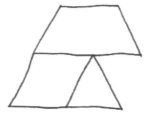

Correct Student Response

All the conditions are satisfied.

Part D

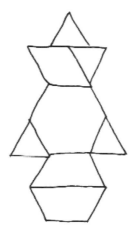

Partially Correct Student Response

The only conditions that are satisfied are using eight pattern blocks and creating a polygon.

Part D

Incorrect Student Response

None of the conditions are met.

Part D

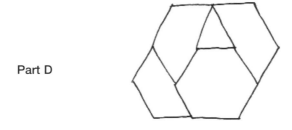

Standard: Analyze characteristics and properties of two- and three-dimensional geometric shapes, and develop mathematical arguments about geometric relationships

Expectation: Classify two- and three-dimensional shapes according to their properties, and develop definitions of classes of shapes, such as triangles and pyramids

5

The two shapes on the square dot paper (below) are alike in some ways and different in other ways. Examine these shapes carefully to find ways they are alike and ways they are different. (Remember all attributes and characteristics of shapes.)

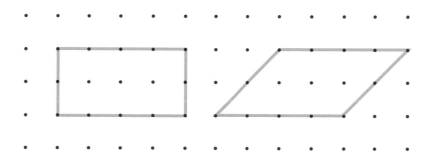

A. Using mathematical language, state three ways these two shapes are alike.

1. _____

2. _____

3. _____

B. Using mathematical language, state three ways these two shapes are different.

1. _____

2. _____

3. _____

About the mathematics: The solution involves using mathematical language to identify shared characteristics of two shapes as well as distinct characteristics of two shapes.

Solution: Some possible answers are the following:
A. Both have opposite sides equal. Both have the same area. Both have the same sum of interior angles. Both have the same number of sides. Both have the same number of angles. Both contain three dots.
B. The perimeters are different. The length of the diagonals is different. One has all right angles. One has acute and obtuse angles. In the second shape not all angles are congruent.

Student Work

Correct Student Response

All similarities and differences are correct.

Part A

1. They both have 8 square blocks inside.
2. They both have 4 angles.
3. They are both parallellogram

Part B

1. The first shape has lines syntry and the other doesn't
2. The first shape has all right angle, the other one dosn't
3. The second shape has acute and obtuse angles the other one dosn't

Partially Correct Student Responses

Response 1

The student correctly notes the similarities, but the ways the shapes are different are incomplete. In addition, "they are not the same shape" does not communicate how the shapes are different.

Part A

1. They have the same area.
2. They have the same length.
3. They have the same height.

Part B

1. They are not the same shape.
2. One of them has 4 right angles.
3. One of them have no right angles.

Response 2

Some of the characteristics are correct. The perimiters of the shapes are different, not the same; also, "sharp corners" is not a mathematical term.

Part A

1. they use up the same area
2. they both are polygons
3. the same perameter

Part B

1. one is not parrelle one is
2. one has right angles one dosen't
3. one has sharp corners one dosen't

Response 3

"Cute angles" is not correct mathematical language.

Part A

1. they both have a line of symetry
2. they are the same with
3. They are both the same length

Part B

1. one has right angles
2. the other has cute angles
3. one has one that has more lines

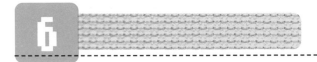

Don had some geometric shapes that he sorted into the following two sets:

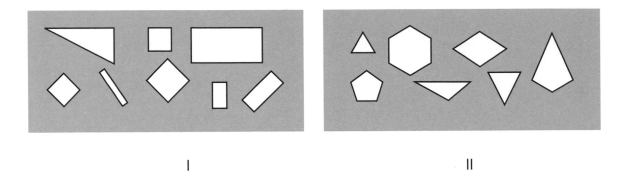

I	II

Explain how you think Don sorted his shapes.

> **About the mathematics:** The solution involves identifying and distinguishing shared characteristics of classes of shapes.
> **Solution:** Possible solution: I—the shapes have at least one right angle; possible solution II—the shapes have no right angles.

Laura was asked to choose 1 of the 3 shapes N, P, and Q that is different from the other 2. Laura chose shape N. Explain how shape N is different from shapes P and Q.

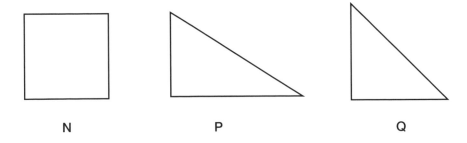

| N | P | Q |

Source: National Assessment of Educational Progress (1996, block 4M10, item 01)

About the mathematics: Students identify distinguishing characteristics of two-dimensional shapes.

Solution: Shape N has more sides and vertices. Shape N is equilateral and equiangular. See student work.

Student Work

Correct Student Response

The student correctly identifies distinguising characteristics.

Answer: _has four sides_

Answer: _The others have 3 points_
N has 4 points

Incorrect Student Responses

Response 1

The student incorrectly identifies shapes P and Q as rectangles rather than as triangles.

Answer: _N shape is square and the other two are rectangles_

Response 2

The student provides characteristics of the letters rather than of the shapes.

Answer: *N is not round anywhere on the letter*

Answer: *a P has a stick with a hoop. N does not have a hoop but Q has a hoop with a stick through it aN does not have a stick through it*

Standard: Analyze characteristics and properties of two- and three-dimensional geometric shapes, and develop mathematical arguments about geometric relationships

Expectation: Investigate, describe, and reason about the results of subdividing, combining, and transforming shapes

8

Draw line segments inside this shape so that the shape is separated into a square, a parallelogram, and an isosceles triangle.

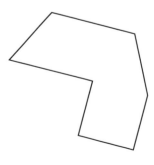

Source: Nova Scotia Elementary Mathematics Program Assessment (2003)
About the mathematics: The solution requires students to reason about subdividing a given shape into other given shapes.
Solution

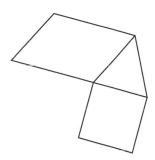

Student Work

Correct Student Responses

All three shapes are clearly visible and correct.

Response 1	Response 2
	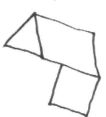

Partially Correct Student Responses

Response 1	Response 2
Two shapes are correct.	One shape is correct.

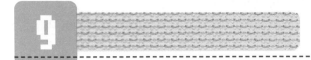

Miguel's teacher gave him a box containing only equilateral triangles. Which figure could he make using only the shapes from his box?

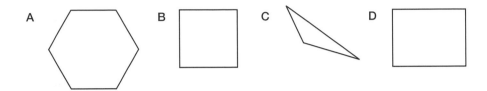

About the mathematics: The solution involves reasoning about subdividing two-dimensional shapes.
Solution: A

For this question you will need to visualize pyramids and prisms.

A. Sue created a net for a regular octagonal pyramid. What types of polygons, and how many of each type, will be on Sue's net?

Use your pattern blocks to complete this question.

B. When you stack pattern blocks of the same color one on top of the other, you get a prism. Joe stacked two pattern blocks of the same color, making a prism with nine edges.

    1. Which pattern block did he use? Answer: _____

    2. What is the name of Joe's prism? Answer: _____

C. Solve this clue puzzle: I am a 3-D shape with five faces. I also have five vertices.
    What shape am I? Answer: _____

Teacher note: This item can be adapted by providing a drawing of a pyramid and a prism.

About the mathematics: The solution requires students to visualize and name three-dimensional shapes and their faces.

Solution: See student work for examples.

    A.   1 regular octagon, 8 congruent isosceles triangles

    B.1. The triangles

    B. 2. Right triangular prism (Note that the term *right* refers to the fact that the prism is a right prism, not that the base shape is a right triangle.)

    C.   Quadrilateral pyramid

Student Work

Correct Student Response

All parts are answered correctly.

Part A   octagon - ① triangle ⑧

Part B 1   triangle

Part B 2   triangular prism

Part C   rectangular pyramid

Partially Correct Student Response

Question A and parts 1 and 2 of question B are answered correctly.

Part A
    octagon 1
    triangles 8

Part B 1
    triangle

Part B 2
    triangular prism

Part C
    pentagonal pyramide

Incorrect Student Response

All parts are answered incorrectly.

Part A
    She used the octagon and she used 4 for her net.

Part B 1
    Square

Part B 2
    Squarebased

Part C
    Squarebased

Standard: Analyze characteristics and properties of two- and three-dimensional geometric shapes, and develop mathematical arguments about geometric relationships

Expectation: Explore congruence and similarity

11

Which of the following sets of shapes is congruent?

A

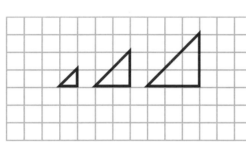

B

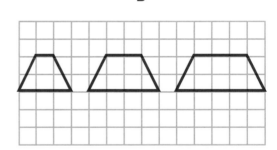

C

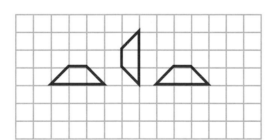

D

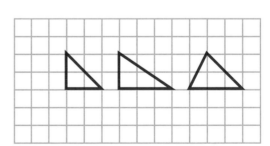

About the mathematics: This item involves identifying congruent shapes.

Solution: C

Standard: Analyze characteristics and properties of two- and three-dimensional geometric shapes and develop mathematical arguments about geometric relationships

Expectation: Make and test conjectures about geometric properties and relationships and develop logical arguments to justify conclusions

12

In the group of polygons drawn below, explain what makes each shape different from the others.

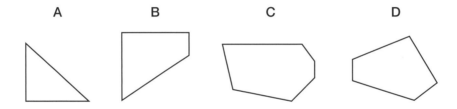

How is each one different?

A. _____

B. _____

C. _____

D. _____

About the mathematics: Students identify distinguishing characteristics among a class of two-dimensional shapes.

Solution
   A. Only shape with line symmetry and three sides
   B. Only shape with two right angles and four sides
   C. Has six sides
   D. Has five sides, and is the only shape that has a United States government building named after it

Standard: Specify locations, and describe spatial relationships using co-ordinate geometry and other representational systems

Expectation: Describe location and movement using common language and geometric vocabulary

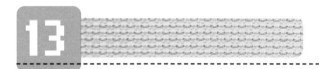

On the grid below, the point at (4, 4) is circled. Circle two other points where the first number is equal to the second number.

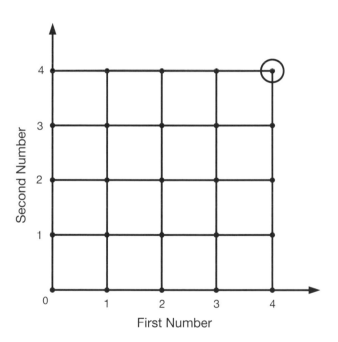

Source: National Assessment of Educational Progress (1992, block 4M15, item 8)

About the mathematics: The solution requires familiarity with coordinate graphing.

Solution: Any two of (0,0), (1,1), (2,2), and (3,3) may be circled.

Standard: Specify locations, and describe spatial relationships using co-ordinate geometry and other representational systems

Expectation: Make and use coordinates systems to specify locations and to describe paths

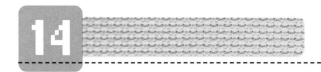

Examine the following geometric shapes.

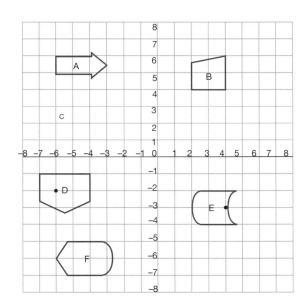

a. In what geometric shape will you find the point $(-5, -2)$?
b. In what geometric shape will you find the point $(3, 5)$?
c. Examine the geometric shape D. What are the coordinates of the black dot inside shape D?
d. Examine the geometric shape E. What are the coordinates of the black dot inside shape E?

About the mathematics: Students correctly identify points in a coordinate plane, given their coordinates; given a point, students correctly identify its coordinates

Solution

    a. D

    b. B

    c. (–6, –2)

    d. (4, –3)

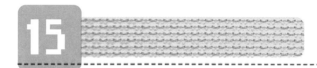

A point is shown on the grid below. The coordinates of the point are (2, 5).

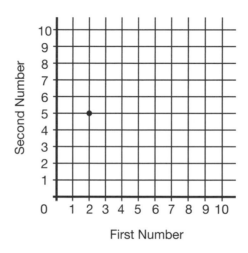

On the same grid draw the point with coordinates (4, 7) and the point with coordinates (8, 0).

Source: National Assessment of Educational Progress (2003, block 4M10, item 10)

About the mathematics: This item involves identifying a point on a coordinate grid, given its coordinates.

Solution: See student work.

Student Work

Correct Student Response

The student correctly graphs the point with coordinates (4, 7) and the point with coordinates (8, 0).

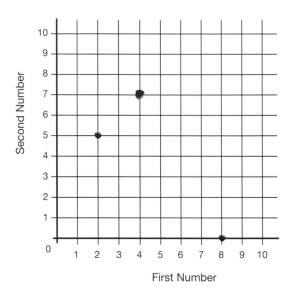

Partially Correct Student Response

The student correctly graphs the point with coordinates (4, 7) but incorrectly graphs the point with coordinates (8, 0) as a point with coordinates (0, 8).

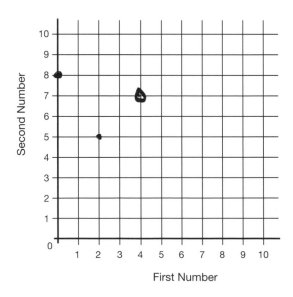

Incorrect Student Response

The student incorrecty graphs both points.

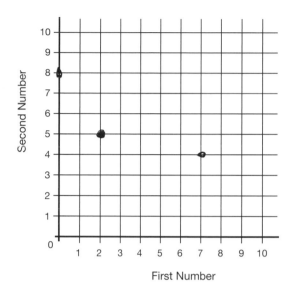

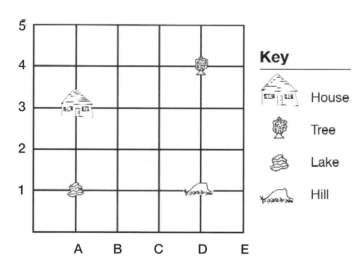

16

On the map below, which ordered pair gives the location of the house?

a. (D, 1)
b. (D, 4)
c. (A, 1)
d. (A, 3)

Key

House

Tree

Lake

Hill

Source: National Assessment of Educational Progress (1990, block 4M7, item 01)
About the mathematics: Given a point, students are asked to give the coordinates in a coordinate plane.
Solution: d

Standard: Specify locations, and describe spatial relationships using co-ordinate geometry and other representational systems

Expectation: Find the distance between points along horizontal and vertical lines of a coordinate system

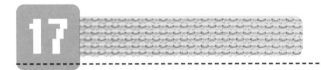

Using the information given at the right, answer the following questions.

A. Mary and her family live in Longsdale. They are going to visit their grandmother. They travel east 20 miles and then north 20 more miles. They stop for lunch. Where did they stop for lunch?

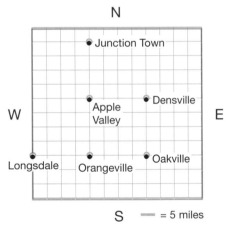

_____

B. After lunch, Mary's father tells the family that grandma's house is not far, it is only 20 miles east. Where is grandma's house? _____

C. Mary's father says, "Before visiting grandma, we will visit Uncle Bob. He lives in Junction Town." How far and in which direction does Uncle Bob lives from where Mary's family stopped for lunch?_____
(In scoring this question, the teacher would mark this last question on the basis of the answer given in question A.)

Source: Adapted from *Balanced Assessment for the Mathematics Curriculum* (Schwartz and Kenney 2000)

About the mathematics: Students must be able to interpret directions on a scale map.

Solution

A. Apple Valley

B. Densville

C. 20 miles north, assuming students gave answer of "Apple Valley" in part A

Standard: Apply transformations and use symmetry to analyze mathematical situations

Expectation: Predict and describe the results of sliding, flipping, and turning two-dimensional shapes

---

18

A student has built this shape out of pattern blocks.

Which of the following represents the result of rotating the student's shape one-quarter turn clockwise around the indicated point?

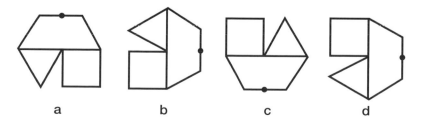

a   b   c   d

Source: Nova Scotia Elementary Mathematics Program Assessment (2003)
About the mathematics: The solution involves the rotation of an object in the plane.
Solution: a

19

If the arrow is rotated one-quarter rotation counterclockwise, to which number will the arrow point?

a. 3
b. 5
c. 8
d. 11

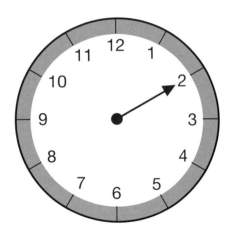

About the mathematics: This item involves the rotation of an object in the plane.
Solution: d

20

Use this diagram of a number line and flag to help you answer the questions.

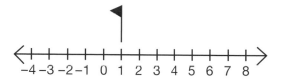

Which shows the result of translating the flag two units to the right and also reflecting it over the line?

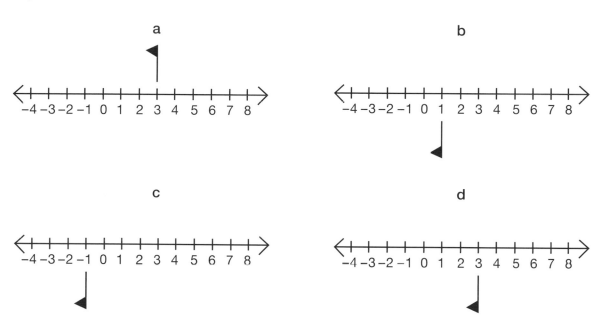

About the mathematics: Students identify the result of a composition of two transformations in the plane.
Solution: d

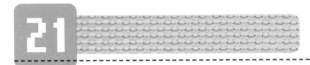

On the grid below you have a trapezoid *ABCD*. Using the center *D*, rotate the trapezoid one-quarter turn counterclockwise. Draw the figure that results on this same grid. Label the points corresponding to *A, B, C, D* as *A', B', C', D',* respectively.

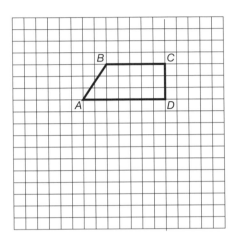

About the mathematics: This item requires an understanding of rotation. It also requires an understanding of counterclockwise in terms of direction.

Solution

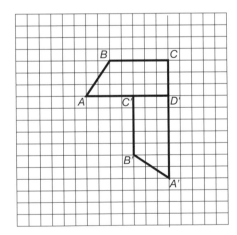

Student Work

Correct Student Response

The student has correctly rotated the trapezoid 90 degrees counterclockwise about *D*.

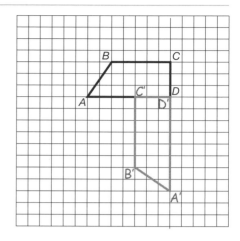

Partially Correct Student Responses

Response 1

The student has correctly rotated the trapezoid but has drawn the trapezoid at an incorrect size.

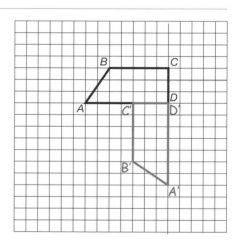

Response 2

The student has correctly rotated the trapezoid but has used the wrong center.

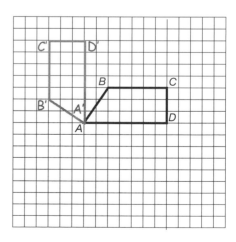

Response 3

The student has used a rotation of 90 degrees, but in the clockwise direction and using the wrong center.

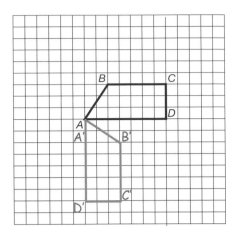

Incorrect Student Response

This student has used the wrong center and used a rotation of less than 90 degrees.

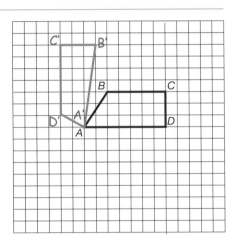

22

Which diagram shows the result of a translation (4 units to the right and 2 units down) of trapezoid *ABCD* to trapezoid *EFGH*?

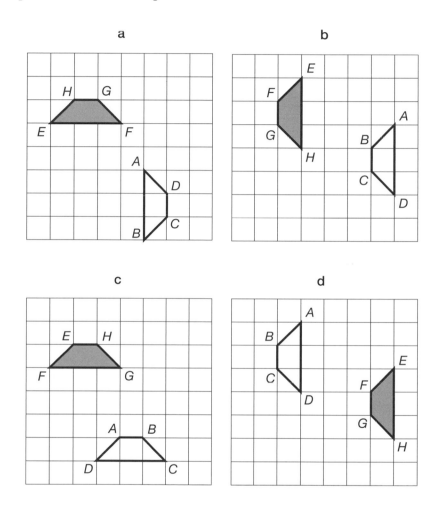

a

b

c

d

About the mathematics: This item involves identifying translations in a plane.

Solution: d

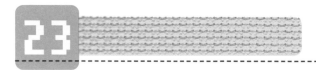

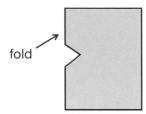

fold

A sheet of paper is folded once, and a piece is cut out as shown above. Which of the following looks like the unfolded paper?

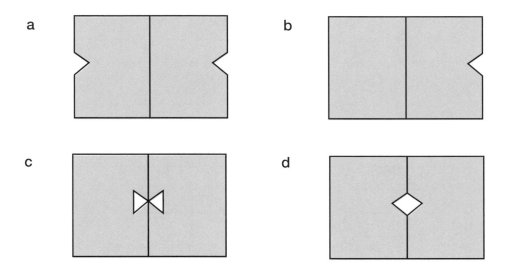

a

b

c

d

Source: National Assessment of Educational Progress (1992, block 4M7, item 04)

About the mathematics: The solution requires visualizing the effects of a cut when paper is unfolded.

Solution: d

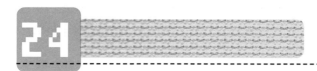

The figure above is shaded on the top side and white on the under side. If the figure were flipped over, its white side could look like which of the following figures?

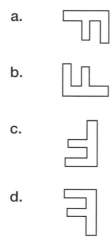

a.

b.

c.

d.

Source: National Assessment of Educational Progress (2003, block 4M6, item 05)
About the mathematics: This item involves the ability to identify a flip (or reflection) in the plane.
Solution: d

Standard: Apply transformation and use symmetry to analyze mathematical situations

Expectation: Identify and describe line and rotational symmetry in two- and three-dimensional shapes and designs

25

On dot paper, a student has made the pentagon and the line segment shown in the diagram below.

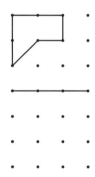

On the same diagram, draw the image of the pentagon reflected over the line segment.

About the mathematics: Students are asked to draw a reflection in the plane.
Solution

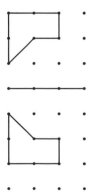

Student Work

Correct Student Response

The student has used the correct reflection, orientation, position, and size.

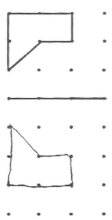

Partially Correct Student Response

The student has used the correct orientation and size but has positioned the pentagon incorrectly.

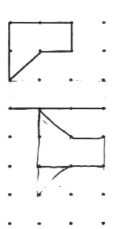

Incorrect Student Responses

Response 1
The student did not use the line segment for the reflection.

Response 2
The student performed a translation.

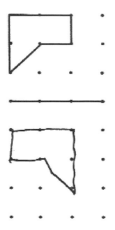

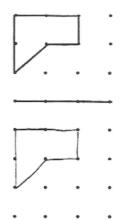

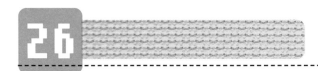

The pattern for the right half of a rug is shown in a rug-making kit as follows:

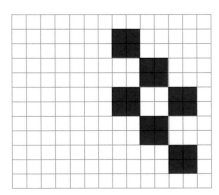

The instructions say that the left side of the rug is a mirror image of the right side. On this grid, draw the left side of the rug.

About the mathematics: The solution involves creating a design with line symmetry and reflecting objects in the plane.

Solution

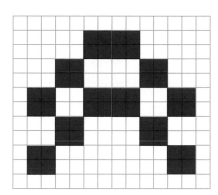

Standard: Use visualization, spatial reasoning, and geometric modeling to solve problems

Expectation: Create and describe mental images of objects, patterns, and paths

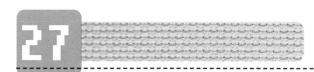

27

Which of the following has the same shape as a cylinder?

a. An egg
b. A book
c. A basketball
d. A can of soup

Source: National Assessment of Educational Progress (1990, block 4M7, item 09)
About the mathematics: Students must connect a geometric term with a real-world example of that object.
Solution: d

Standard: Use visualization, spatial reasoning, and geometric modeling to solve problems

Expectation: Identify and build a three-dimensional object from two-dimensional representations of that object

28

Which of the following could NOT be folded into a cube?

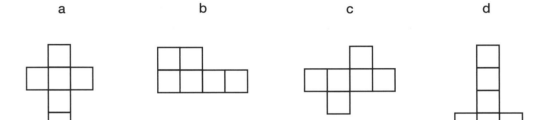

a   b   c   d

Source: National Assessment of Educational Progress (2003, block 4M6, item 14)

About the mathematics: This item involves visualizing a cube, given its net.

Solution: b

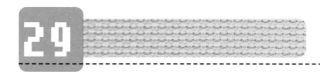

The squares in the figure below represent the faces of a cube that has been cut along some edges and flattened. When the original cube was resting on face X, which face was on top?

a. Face A
b. Face B
c. Face C
d. Face D

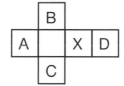

Source: National Assessment of Educational Progress (1992, block 4M5, item 14)

About the mathematics: This item involves visualizing a cube, given a net.

Solution: a

Standard: Use visualization, spatial reasoning, and geometric modeling to solve problems

Expectation: Recognize geometric ideas and relationships and apply them to other disciplines and to problems that arise in the classroom or in everyday life

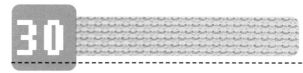

A cow is tied to a post in the middle of a flat meadow. If the cow's rope is several meters long, which of the following figures shows the shape of the region where the cow can graze?

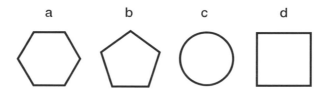

Source: National Assessment of Educational Progress (2003, block 4M10, item 14)
About the mathematics: The solution involves connecting a given context with a geometric shape that would result from that context.
Solution: c

31

According to the map in the figure below, which streets appear to be parallel to each other?

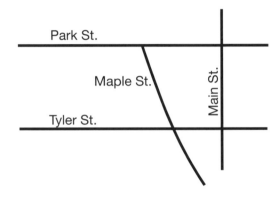

a. Park and Main
b. Tyler and Maple
c. Park and Tyler
d. Main and Tyler

Source: National Assessment of Educational Progress, 1990, block 4M7, item 8
About the mathematics: The solution involves identifying parallel lines in the context of a street map.
Solution: c

Measurement

Measurement is a process that students in grades 3–5 use every day as they explore questions related to their school or home environment. For example, how much catsup is used in the school cafeteria each day? What is the distance from my house to the school? What is the range of heights of players on the basketball team? Such questions require students to use concepts and tools of measurement to collect data and to describe and quantify their world. In grades 3–5, measurements help connect ideas within areas of mathematics and between mathematics and other disciplines. It can serve as a context to help students understand important mathematical concepts such as fractions, geometric shapes, and ways of describing data.

In grades 3–5, students should deepen and expand their understanding and use of measurement. For example, they should measure other attributes such as area and angle. They need to begin paying closer attention to the degree of accuracy when measuring and use a wider variety of measurement tools. They should also begin to develop and use formulas for the measurement of certain attributes, such as area.

In learning about measurement and learning how to measure, students should be actively involved, drawing on familiar and accessible contexts. For example, students in grades 3–5 should measure objects and space in their classroom or use maps to determine locations and distances around their community. They should determine an appropriate unit and use it to measure the area of their classroom's floor, estimate the time it takes to do various tasks, and measure and represent change in the size of attributes, such as their height.

—National Council of Teachers of Mathematics [1]

---

1 National Council of Teachers of Mathematics (2000, p. 171)

THE ASSESSMENT tasks in this strand are designed to illuminate students' understanding of the concepts recommended by the NCTM Measurement Standards for grades 3–5. The tasks are designed to inform teachers of their students' knowledge of measurement, including the conventions and processes of measurement. Open-response questions are again included to help teachers assess students' ability to communicate mathematical concepts in writing and to represent mathematical ideas in a variety of forms.

Measurement Assessment Items

Standard: Understand measurable attributes of objects and the units, systems, and processes of measurement

Expectation: Understand such attributes as length, area, weight, volume, and size of angle and select the appropriate type of unit for measuring each attribute

1

Which of these instruments best measures each of the following?

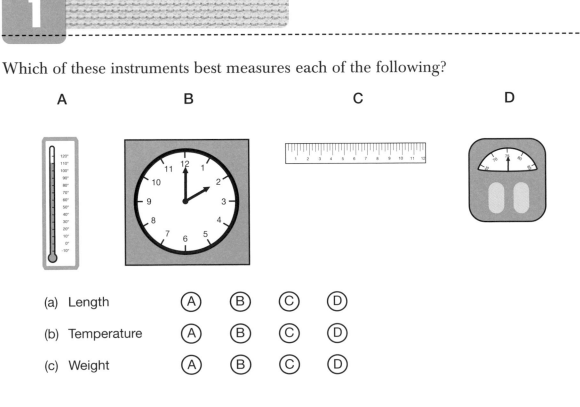

	A	B	C	D
(a) Length	Ⓐ	Ⓑ	Ⓒ	Ⓓ
(b) Temperature	Ⓐ	Ⓑ	Ⓒ	Ⓓ
(c) Weight	Ⓐ	Ⓑ	Ⓒ	Ⓓ

Teacher note: This item assesses a student's ability to match the appropriate measuring tool with the type of measurement required. Since only three types of measurement are listed, you might ask students, "What kind of measurement would you make with the tool left over?"

Source: National Assessment of Educational Progress (1996, block 4M9, item 02)

About the mathematics: This item requires measuring an attribute by using an appropriate unit and tool.

Solution: Length is best measured by C (ruler), temperature is best measured by A (thermometer), and weight is best measured by D (scale).

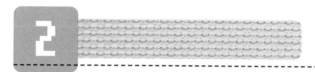

Four children measured the width of a room by counting the number of paces they took to cross it. The chart shows their measurements.

Name	Number of Paces
Stephen	10
Erlane	8
Ana	9
Carlos	7

Who had the longest pace?

How do you know?

Source: Adapted from Trends in International Mathematics and Science Study (1999, item L12)

About the mathematics: A large unit (in this instance, paces) requires fewer repetitions than a smaller unit in covering the same distance.

About the mathematics: This item requires students to identify length using the informal measure of a pace.

Solution: Carlos

What is the temperature reading shown on the thermometer?

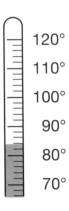

Source: National Assessment of Educational Progress (2003, block 4M10, item 13)

About the mathematics: This item involves reading a thermometer.

Solution: 84°

On the map, 1 cm represents 10 km on the land. On the land, about how far apart are the towns Melville and Folley?

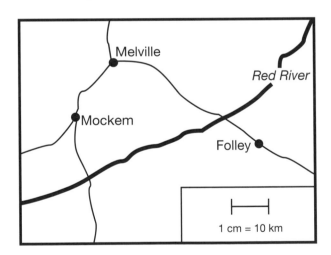

a.   5 km
b. 30 km
c. 40 km
d. 50 km

Source: Trends in International Mathematics and Science Study (1999, item J18)

About the mathematics: This item assesses students' ability to use standard metric units for linear measurement.

Solution: d

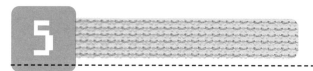

The car is 3.5m long. About how long is the building?

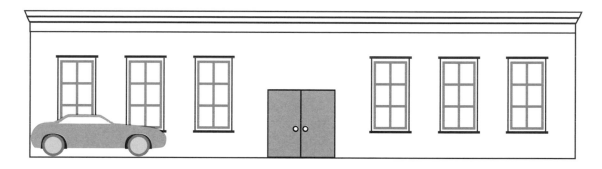

a. 18m

b. 14m

c. 10m

d. 4m

Source: Trends in International Mathematics and Science Study (1999, item L09)

About the mathematics: For this item, students use an object of known length to estimate linear measurement.

Solution: b

6

On the grid below, draw a rectangle with an area of 12 square units, and justify your answer.

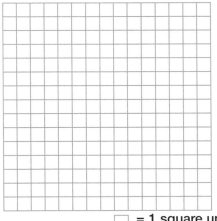

☐ = 1 square unit

Source: Adapted from National Assessment of Educational Progress (1992, block 4M7, item 02)

About the mathematics: This item requires familiarity with rectangles and area.

Solution: Different solutions are possible. The explanation should reflect an understanding of area comprising twelve squares.

Student Work

Correct student response

On the grid below, draw a rectangle with an area of 12 square units.

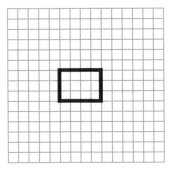

Incorrect student responses

Response 1	Response 2
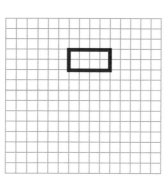	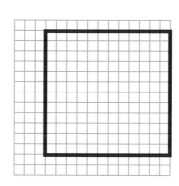

Teacher note: The student work for this item provides an opportunity for discussion of error analysis. For example, the first incorrect student work sample has a perimeter of 12, so the student may have confused area and perimeter.

Which angle in the figure has a measurement closest to 45°

a. *p*
b. *q*
c. *r*
d. *s*

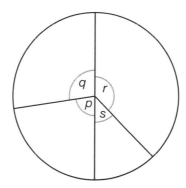

How do you know?

Source: Adapted from Trends in International Mathematics and Science Study (1999, item N15)

About the mathematics: This item requires familiarity with degrees in measuring angles. The student should recognize a 90-degree angle and use it as a benchmark to estimate the measure of other angles.

Solution: d

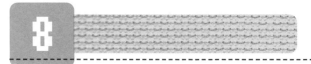

Brett needs to cut a piece of string into four equal pieces without using a ruler or other measuring instrument.

Write directions that will explain to Brett how to do this.

> **Source:** National Assessment of Educational Progress (1996, block 4M12, item 08)
>
> **About the mathematics:** This item requires students to reason though the process of using nonstandard measuring tools to find a fractional part of a whole.
>
> **Solution:** Fold the string into two equal or congruent lengths. Cut the string at the fold. Next, fold each of the cut pieces of string into two equal or congruent lengths. Cut the string at the fold. The result will be four equivalent lengths of string.

Student Work

Correct student responses

Response 1

> Fold it untill the makes two equal parts cut it. Then fold it again cut it

Response 2

> Fold it in half once then fold it equally again. Cut the second then cut the first.

124

Partially correct student responses

Response 1

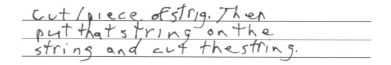

Cut them to half
put them sid by side and cut again

Response 2

Cut / piece of strig. Then
put that string on the
string and cut the string.

Incorrect student responses

Response 1

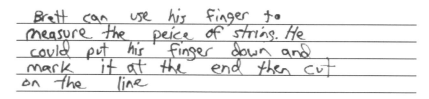

Brett can use his finger to
measure the peice of string. He
could put his finger down and
mark it at the end then cut
on the line

Response 2

measure how long it is then see what equals
that fair times then cut it.

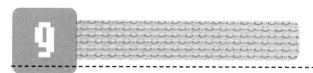

9

In the space below, draw an angle that is larger than 90° and an angle that is smaller than 90°.

Label both angles.

About the mathematics: A successful solution requires familiarity with degrees in measuring angles; the knowledge that 90 degrees forms a right angle is also useful.

Solution: Answers will vary; the following are examples:

Greater than 90°   Less than 90°

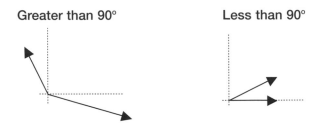

Standard: Understand measurable attributes of objects and the units, systems, and processes of measurement

Expectation: Understand the need for measuring with standard units, and become familiar with standard units in the customary and metric systems

10

Use your centimeter ruler to make the following measurements to the nearest centimeter.

What is the length of one of the longer sides of the rectangle?

Answer:

_____

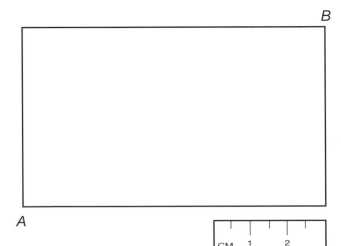

Teacher note: This item works well in communicating to students the need to label units. Before this item is used, students should be aware of the rubric that will be used to assess it.

Source: Adapted from National Assessment of Educational Progress (1992, block 4M5, item 10)

About the mathematics: Measuring the length of the longer side requires students to read a ruler.

Solution: 8 cm

Rubric: 2 points for answer of 8 cm
1 point for answer of 8 (with no label or an incorrect label)
0 point for any answer different from 8

Student Work

Correct student responses
2 points

Response 1	Response 2
Answer: _____ 8cm _____	Answer: _____ 8 cenimeters _____

Incorrect student responses
0 points

Response 1	Response 2
Answer: _____ 3 _____	Answer: _____ 6 _____

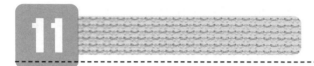

What is the length of the toothpick in the figure below?

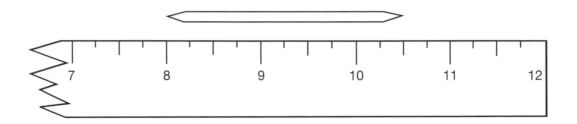

Source: National Assessment of Educational Progress (2003, block 4M6, item 18)

About the mathematics: Reading a ruler

Solution: 2.5 inches

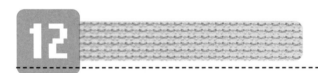

Which of these would most likely be measured in milliliters?

a. The amount of liquid in a teaspoon
b. The weight (mass) of a pin
c. The amount of gasoline in a tank
d. The thickness of 10 sheets of paper

Source: Trends in International Mathematics and Science Study (1999, item N7)

About the mathematics: Students should realize that, in addition to sharing the characteristic of the attribute being measured, a unit is most useful when it is appropriate—that is, can provide a satisfactorily accurate measurement. (For example, the amount of gasoline in a tank could be measured in milliliters, but the result would be more precise than is typically necessary; a unit such as liters or gallons would be more appropriate.)

Solution: a

13

What is the approximate area of the figure drawn on the square dot paper below?

Explain how you estimated the area.

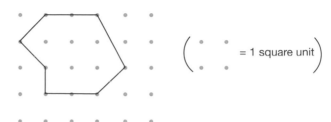

Source: *Nova Scotia Elementary Mathematics Program Assessment* (2003)

About the mathematics: Students use a square unit to find the area of irregular polygons.

Solution: An answer between 8 square units and 9 square units is acceptable.

Rubric: Add the points for the answer and the explanation to determine the total score.

Answer:

1 point	Answers between 8 and 9 square units
0.5 point	Answer less than 8 or greater than 9
0 point	All other answers

Explanation:

2 points	Correct answer with complete and clear explanation of a correct strategy. (The two most likely strategies are these: [a] inside the shape, counting full square units; combining partial square units to make other full square units; and adding these amounts together; and [b] enclosing shape in a 3 × 4 rectangle, counting full square units and combining partial square units to make full square units between the given shape and the 3 × 4 rectangle, and subtracting the total of these from 12 square units.)
1.5 point	Same as for 2.0 *except* for inaccurate wording and/or misuse of words (e.g., student uses *half* when he or she means *part*)
1.0 point	An explanation that suggests counting squares inside the shape but makes no discrimination between full squares and combinations of partial squares
0.5 point	Any other explanation indicating that the student knows that area is the region inside the shape
0 point	Other explanations or an answer with no explanation

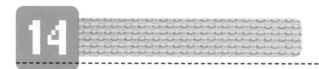

If the string in the diagram is pulled straight, which of these is closest to its length?

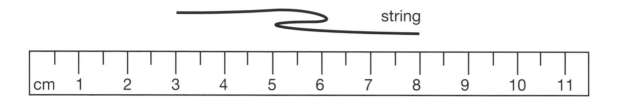

a. 5 cm
b. 6 cm
c. 7 cm
d. 8 cm

How do you know?

Source: Adapted from Trends in International Mathematics and Science Study (1999, item P12)

About the mathematics: In addition to dealing with the "doubled over" part of the string, this problem requires accurately reading a ruler.

Solution: c

Standard: Understand measurable attributes of objects and the units, systems, and processes of measurement

Expectation: Carry out simple unit conversions, such as from centimeters to meters, within a system of measurement

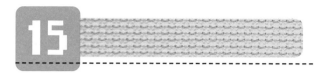

A measurement of 60 inches is equal to how many feet?

(12 INCHES = 1 FOOT)

Answer: _____

A measurement of 72 inches is how many yards?

(3 FEET = 1 YARD)

Answer: _____

> **About the mathematics:** This item involves conversions using customary measures.
> **Solution:** 5 feet; 2 yards

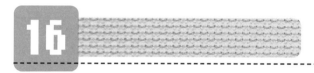

At a picnic cider is served in cups. If 1 pint will fill 2 cups, how many cups can be filled from 8 pints of cider? Show all your work.

How do you know?

> **Source:** Adapted from National Assessment of Educational Progress (2003, block 4M7, item 8)
> **About the mathematics:** The solution involves conversion using customary measures.
> **Solution:** 16 cups

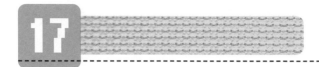

If the large pitcher was full, 2 of the small pitchers could be filled from it.
If the small pitcher was full, 4 of these glasses could be filled from it.

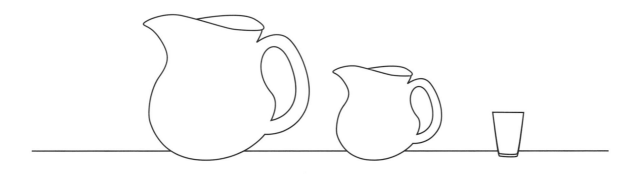

Suppose the large pitcher was filled with milk. How many of the glasses could be filled from it?

Show all your work.

> **Source:** *Nova Scotia Elementary Mathematics Program Assessment* (2003)
> **About the mathematics:** The solution involves determining conversions with nonstandard units.
> **Solution:** Two small pitchers hold the same as 1 large pitcher, 4 glasses hold the same as 1 small pitcher, 8 glasses hold the same as 2 small pitchers, so 8 glasses hold the same as 1 large pitcher.

Standard: Understand measurable attributes of objects and the units, systems, and processes of measurement

Expectation: Understand that measurements are approximations, and understand how differences in units affect precision

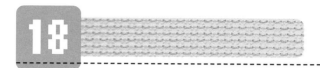

Using a centimeter ruler like this one,

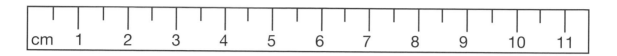

you can measure accurately to the nearest

a. millimeter
b. half-millimeter
c. centimeter
d. half-centimeter

> **Teacher note:** This item can be adapted by changing the ruler to one marked in increments of 1/2 inch, 1/4 inch, or 1/8 inch or increments of 1/10 cm.
> **Source:** Trends in International Mathematics and Science Study (1999, item F10)
> **About the mathematics:** This item requires understanding the precision of units of measure on a metric ruler.
> **Solution:** d

Rudy takes a 2-mile walk along a nature trail. Which of the following is a reasonable amount of time for Rudy to take to walk the trail?

a. 60 seconds
b. 60 minutes
c. 60 hours
d. 60 days

Source: National Assessment of Educational Progress (2003, block 4M7, item 02)

About the mathematics: Students must be able to match distance and time reasonably.

Solution: b

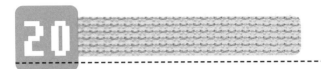

Linda had three large boxes all the same size and three different kinds of balls as shown below. If she fills each box with the kind of balls shown, which box will have the fewest balls?

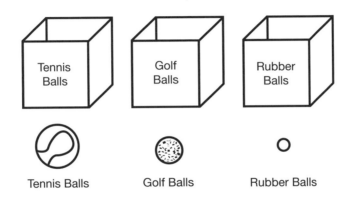

| Tennis Balls | Golf Balls | Rubber Balls |

a. The box with the tennis balls
b. The box with the golf balls
c. The box with the rubber balls
d. You can't tell.

Explain how you know?

Teachers note: Extend this item by asking which box will have the most balls, and why.

Source: Adapted from National Assessment of Educational Progress (1990, grade 4, block 4M7, item 07)

About the mathematics: The solution involves estimating volume with different units.

Solution: a

21

Mr. Larson is planning to buy one of these kinds of tile for his bathroom floor.

Tile 1   Tile 2   Tile 3

Which tile would he need the most of to completely cover the floor?

Justify your answer.

> **Source:** *Nova Scotia Elementary Mathematics Program Assessment* (2003)
> **About the mathematics:** The solution involves estimating area with different units.
> **Solution:** Tile 2

22

Which bag of fruit weighs the most?

a. There is not enough information given to tell.
b. The bag of lemons
c. The bag of apples
d. The bag of grapefruit

Explain your answer:

Source: *Nova Scotia Elementary Mathematics Program Assessment* (2003)
About the mathematics: This item involves reasoning about comparisons of weights.
Solution: a

Standard: Understand measurable attributes of objects and the units, systems, and processes of measurement

Expectation: Explore what happens to measurements of a two-dimensional shape, such as its perimeter and area, when the shape is changed in some way

If both the square and the triangle below have the same perimeter, what is the length of each side of the square?

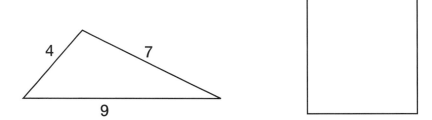

Justify your answer.

Source: Adapted from Trends in International Mathematics and Science Study (1999, item L13)
About the mathematics: Students reason about the perimeter of a given shape.
Solution: 5 units. The perimeter of the triangle is 20, and because a square is equilateral, each side will measure 20 ÷ 4, or 5, units.

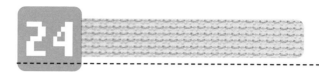

One rectangle with an area of 36 square units is shown below.

Find as many other ways as you can to arrange 36 square units in a rectangle. Using pictures or words, explain how you now that the area of each of your rectangles is 36 square units.

Source: *Nova Scotia Elementary Mathematics Program Assessment* (2003)

About the mathematics: The solution involves determining all possible rectangular arrays with 36 square units.

Solution: 1 × 36 rectangle, 2 × 18 rectangle, 3 × 12 rectangle, 4 × 9 rectangle (the one shown in the problem), 6 × 6 rectangle

Teacher note: Anticipate questions from students about whether 4 rows with 9 tiles in each is the same array as a rectangle with 9 rows with 4 tiles in each. For the purpose of finding all possibilities, the easiest approach is to consider them the same, because the rectangle with 4 rows of 9 tiles each can be rotated to obtain the rectangle with 9 rows of 4 tiles. Also anticipate the need to discuss whether a square is a rectangle, once the dimensions 6 × 6 are proposed.

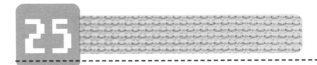

The rectangle shown is twice as long as it is wide.

What is the ratio of the width of the rectangle to the perimeter?

a. $\frac{1}{2}$
b. $\frac{1}{3}$
c. $\frac{1}{4}$
d. $\frac{1}{6}$

Justify your answer.

> **Teacher note:** This item could be changed to an open-ended item with direction to "show your work." It could also be adapted by changing the dimensions of the rectangle (e.g., a rectangle that is three times as long as it is wide).
> **Source:** Adapted from Trends in International Mathematics and Science Study (1999, item N8)
> **About the mathematics:** This item requires students to think about the perimeter of the rectangle in terms of the unit "width of rectangle."
> **Solution:** d

Mrs. Bush has a garden that measures 8 feet by 10 feet. She wants to extend her

garden to be 9 feet by 11 feet. Describe the perimeter and area of each garden, and compare the perimeter and area of the original garden with those of the new garden.

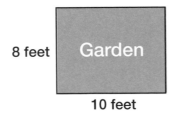

8 feet   Garden

10 feet

About the mathematics: This item involves finding changes in the area and perimeter of a rectangle when its dimensions change.

Solution: The original garden had an area of 80 square feet and a perimeter of 36 feet. The enlarged garden has an area of 99 square feet and a perimeter of 40 feet. The extended garden has an area that is 19 square feet more than that of the original garden. The extended garden has a perimeter that is 4 feet more than that of the original garden.

Standard: Apply appropriate techniques, tools, and formulas to determine measurements

Expectation: Develop strategies for estimating the perimeters, areas, and volumes of irregular shapes

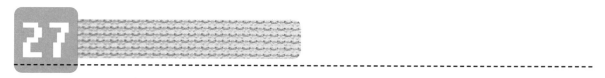

How many of the right triangles are needed to cover the surface of the rectangle?

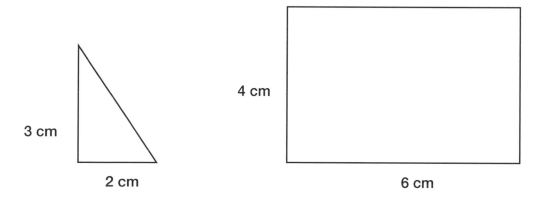

3 cm

2 cm

4 cm

6 cm

Justify your answer.

About the mathematics: The solution involves measuring area with a non-standard unit.
Solution: 8 right triangles are needed.

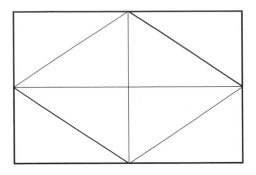

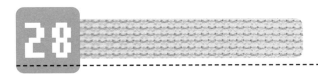

Which figure has the smallest area?

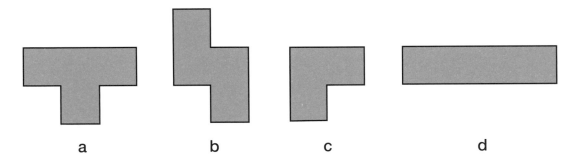

| a | b | c | d |

Justify your answer.

Source: Adapted from National Assessment of Educational Progress (1992, block 4M15, item 02)
About the mathematics: This item requires students to estimate area.
Solution: c; the answer can be seen by sketching in square units, for example, for c:

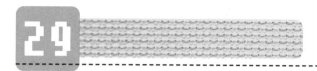

The volume of the following cube is 1 cubic centimeter. All spaces for missing cubes are shown in the figure.

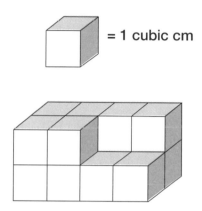

= 1 cubic cm

What is the volume of this figure?

Source: Adapted from Massachusetts Comprehensive Assessment System (release of spring 2000 test items, p. 123, item 12)

About the mathematics: This item involves visualizing a three-dimensional object from a two-dimensional representation; it also requires an understanding of volume.

Solution: 14 cubic cm

Teacher note: This item can be made more accessible, particularly for English language learners, by using blocks and constructing the figure. The item can be made more challenging by increasing the dimensions and changing the blocks that are removed.

30

The City Park Committee wants to fence in an area of the neighborhood park for young children to use as a playground. It has 12 sections of fence. Each section of fence is one unit long.

A. On the grid below draw *4 different* closed shapes using all 12 sections of fence for each of the shapes.

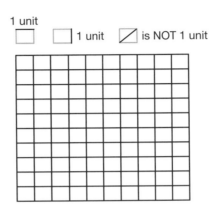

1 unit

☐ ☐ 1 unit ▱ is NOT 1 unit

B. What is the *area* of each of your shapes? *Write the area inside each shape.*

C. Decide which shape would be the best one for a playground. *Circle your choice.* Explain why this is the best shape for a playground.

> **Source:** Adapted from Massachusetts Comprehensive Assessment System (release of May 1998 test items, p. 128, item 30)
> **About the mathematics:** The solution involves finding areas of different shapes having the same area.
> **Solution:** Answers will vary.

31

The following are maps of two lakes. Describe a way to estimate the area of both lakes. You may not cut out the pictures or fold the paper. Use your method to estimate the areas of both lakes.

Source: Adapted from *Nova Scotia Elementary Mathematics Program Assessment* (2003)

About the mathematics: Students estimate area given the approximate length of one side of a shape.

Solution: Answers will vary. Lake Willa is about 12 square kilometers because it appears to be about 6 km long; Moon Lake is approximately 9 square kilometers because each side appears to be about 3 kilometers long.

Standard: Apply appropriate techniques, tools, and formulas to determine measurements

Expectation: Select and apply appropriate standard units and tools to measure length, area, volume, weight, time, temperature, and the size of angles

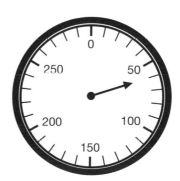

What is the weight shown on the scale?

a. 6 pounds
b. 7 pounds
c. 51 pounds
d. 60 pounds

Source: Trends in International Mathematics and Science Study (1999, item L13)
About the mathematics: This item involves determining scale on a measuring instrument.
Solution: d

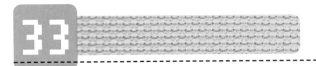

The weight (mass) of a clothespin is 9.2 grams. Which of the following is the best estimate of the total weight (mass) of 1000 clothespins?

a. 900 grams
b. 9,000 grams
c. 90,000 grams
d. 900,000 grams

Justify your answer.

Source: Adapted from Trends in International Mathematics and Science Study (1999, item L6)
About the mathematics: This item requires an understanding of approximations and place value.
Solution: b. Because 1 clothespin weighs approximately 9 grams, 1000 clothespins will weigh approximately 1000 × 9, or 9000, grams.

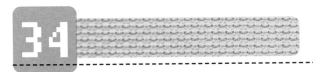

The first time Ms. Anderson's class visited the science display, they left the classroom at the time shown on the clock [at the right]. They returned to the classroom 55 minutes later. What time did they return to the classroom?

Source: Trends in International Mathematics and Science Study (1999, item N15)

About the mathematics: This item involves the measurement of time.

Solution: 2:10

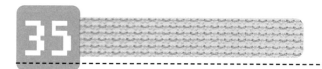

In the figure below, how many small cubes were put together to form the large cube?

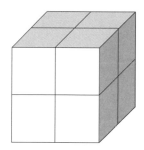

Teacher note: This item can be adapted by using a 3 × 3 × 3 cube. Providing blocks for students to use would make items like this more accessible to students, particularly for English language learners.

Source: National Assessment of Educational Progress (1996, block 4M9, item 6)

About the mathematics: The solution involves visualization of a three-dimensional shape with only part of the individual components visible.

Solution: Eight cubes were used.

36

The Celsius temperature rose from 4 degrees above zero to the temperature shown on the thermometer at the right. How many degrees did the temperature rise?

Justify your answer.

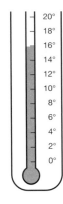

Source: Adapted from National Assessment of Educational Progress (2003, block 4M7, item 13)

About the mathematics: This item assesses students' ability to read a thermometer and determine the range of temperature change.

Solution: The temperature rose 12 degrees; 16 degrees – 4 degrees = 12 degrees.

37

This table shows temperatures at various times on four days.

Temperature

	6 A.M.	9 A.M.	Noon	3 P.M.	6 P.M.
Monday	15	17	24	21	16
Tuesday	20	16	15	10	9
Wednesday	8	14	16	19	15
Thursday	8	11	19	26	20

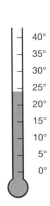

On which day and at what time was the temperature shown in the table the same as that shown on the thermometer?

Justify your answer.

Source: Adapted from Trends in International Mathematics and Science Study (1999, item P16)
About the mathematics: This item involves reading thermometer and interpreting a table.
Solution: Monday at noon

38

There are 24 pieces of candy in a box that is 4 inches long, 3 inches wide, and 2 inches high. Each piece of candy takes up 1 inch by 1 inch by 1 inch. List the dimensions for 3 other boxes that will hold exactly 24 pieces of candy.

Justify your answer.

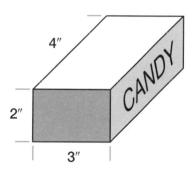

About the mathematics: This item requires an understanding that certain quantities can be organized in various ways.
Solution: Correct solutions include 1 inch wide, 1 inch high, 24 inches long; 1 inch wide, 3 inches high, 8 inches long; 2 inches high, 4 inches wide, 3 inches long (others answers are possible).

Standard: Apply appropriate techniques, tools, and formulas to determine measurements

Expectation: Select and use benchmarks to estimate measurements

39

Describe how you can estimate the number of beads in the full glass.

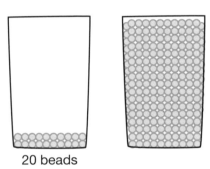

20 beads

About the mathematics: This item assesses students' ability to use a benchmark to estimate volume.

Solution: Two possibilities: count the number of double layers of beads in the full glass, and multiply that number by 20 to obtain an estimate of the number of beads in the full glass; or count the number of single layers in the full glass, and multiply that number by 10.

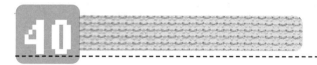

The container on the left was filled with sand. Kyle took one tumbler of sand out of the container. How many more tumblers could he fill with the sand remaining in the container on the left?

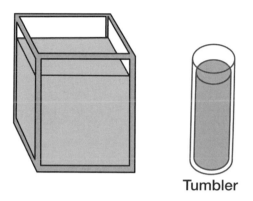

Tumbler

Explain how you found your answer.

> **Source:** *Nova Scotia Elementary Mathematics Program Assessment* (2003)
> **About the mathematics:** This item involves the estimation of volume.
> **Solution:** 5 or 6 tumblers. Because the question calls for an estimate, answers may vary slightly.

Standard: Apply appropriate techniques, tools, and formulas to determine measurements

Expectation: Develop, understand, and use formulas to find the area of rectangles and related triangles and parallelograms

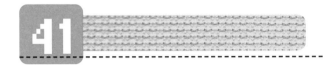

The figure shows a shaded rectangle inside a parallelogram. What is the area of the shaded rectangle?

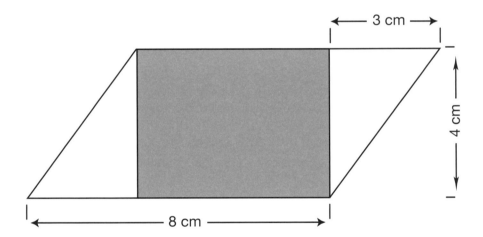

Answer: _____

Justify your answer.

> **Source:** Adapted from Trends in International Mathematics and Science Study (1999, item TO3)
> **About the mathematics:** The solution involves determining the area of a rectangle.
> **Solution:** 20 cm²

A rectangular garden that is next to a building has a path around the other three sides, as shown. Find the area of the path surrounding the garden.

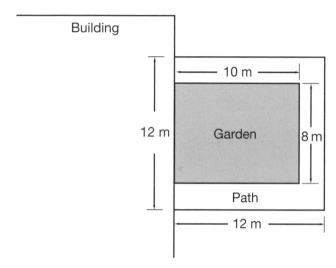

What is the area of the path?

Describe how you might find the area of the garden.

Source: Adapted from Trends in International Mathematics and Science Study (1999, item J10)

About the mathematics: This item involves finding the areas of rectangular shapes.

Solution: The path is 64 square meters. To find the area of the garden, multiply the width of 8 meters by the length of 10 meters for an area of 80 square meters.

Standard: Develop strategies to determine the surface areas and volumes of rectangular solids

Expectation: Apply appropriate techniques, tools, and formulas to determine measurements

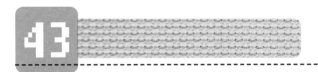

Cindy has put four cubes into this container.

About how many of these cubes will the container hold?

a. About 4
b. About 9
c. About 16
d. About 27

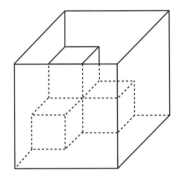

Explain how you found the answer.

> **Source:** *Nova Scotia Elementary Mathematics Program Assessment* (2003)
> **About the mathematics:** Students develop strategies to determine the volume of a rectangular solid.
> **Solution:** d. The diagram suggests that one more cube can be placed across the back of the container, one more cube can be placed in front of the two cubes on the bottom, and one more can be placed on top of the cubes already in the container. If so, then the volume is 3 × 3 × 3, for a total volume of 27 cubes.

5

Data Analysis and Probability

DATA ANALYSIS and probability is an area of mathematics that children seem to readily identify with as it relates to their own lives. Graphs dominate the pages of their history and science books. Students are deluged with information that they must interpret. The use and abuse of statistical information are constantly being presented to students through television and printed advertisements. Often, advertisements present misleading opinions and trends that students must decipher. NCTM's *Principles and Standards for School Mathematics* states, "Students need to know about data analysis and related aspects of probability in order to reason statistically—skills necessary to becoming an informed citizen and an intelligent consumer."[1]

A child's curiosity about his or her environment leads to a natural interest in gathering, analyzing, and representing data. Data can answer questions about, for example, which kind of soda the class likes best and then help make the decision of which kind to buy for the next party. Probability measures possible occurrences of events to predict outcomes, such as whether orange soda is equally as likely to be drunk as grape soda.

Careful reading of the Data Analysis and Probability strand will give the teacher information about students' learning to reason statistically. As concepts and procedures become more sophisticated across the grades, teachers can predict that the chances of preparing students who will grow to be informed citizens and intelligent consumers will be highly likely.

---

1 National Council of Teachers of Mathematics (2000, p. 171)

Data Analysis and Probability Assessment Items

Standard: Formulate questions that can be addressed with data and collect, organize, and display relevant data to answer them

Expectation: Design investigations to address a question and consider how data-collection methods affect the nature of the data set

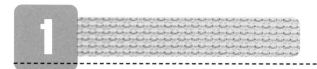

A teacher brought a large jar of animal crackers to school. He said that each student would be allowed to take one handful of animal crackers for snack time. Travis thought this was a great idea, but Margaret thought it was unfair because her hand was a lot smaller than most students' hands. Travis and the teacher then had to agree with Margaret. Write a way in which to determine a fair serving of animal crackers using either hand size or some other method.

> **Source:** Adapted from Exemplars (fall 1999)
>
> **About the mathematics:** Students design investigations to address a question, and consider how data collection methods affect the nature of the data set.
>
> **Solution:** Answers will vary. The following are two possible solutions: A. The students could take turns handing out the animal crackers. In this way, every child would get a chance to distribute the crackers, but because only one child would do so each day, the portions would be about the same size. B. The animal crackers could be placed into a small paper drinking cup designed for a dispenser. Since all the paper cups in the dispenser stack are about the same size, each child would get about the same amount of animal crackers.

Standard: Formulate questions that can be addressed with data and collect, organize, and display relevant data to answer them

Expectation: Collect data using observations, surveys, and experiments

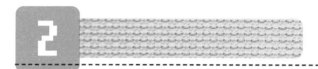

A principal wants to know how many cars drive by the school in the hour after school is out. What is the best way for her to find out? Justify your answer.

a. Ask the teachers
b. Stand on the street and count the cars
c. Ask the people in the neighborhood
d. Call the transportation department

> **Source:** Adapted from *Principles and Standards for School Mathematics* (NCTM 2000, p. 178)
> **About the mathematics:** This item involves collecting data using observations.
> **Solution:** b. This type of data is best gathered by observation. Collecting data for a week or so would generate the best data.

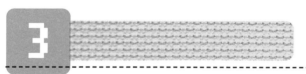

How can you find out how 4th graders spend their time after school?

- Create a plan to collect information in order to answer this question.
- Who would you ask?
- Who wouldn't you ask? Explain.
- How would you record your data?

Source: *Principles and Standards for School Mathematics* (NCTM 2000, p. 178)

About the mathematics: Students design an investigation; formulate questions; and collect, represent, summarize, and interpret data.

Solution: Answers will vary. See the student work that follows the rubric.

Rubric

Points Possible	Description	Points Awarded
1	Data sampling is of 4th graders	
1	Ask each person what they do, or give her or him a short list of activities to choose from	
1	Records data in a tally chart with after-school activities, or makes a list of students and writes an activity or activities next to each name	
1	Organizes data in a bar graph or pie graph	
4	**Total number of points**	

Student Work

Correct student response

First you would gather data by asking the 4th graders what they do in their free time. Then, you put the data in groups. Last you make the data into a bar graph.

Partial student response—sample not defined

• My plan will be to ask kids if they play baseball, practices, Karate, the library or if they just go straight home. I would ask every person what they do and....

• I would use a bar graph or tallies I would write down the topic and tally the total to see which was the most reasonable thing to do after school.

Incomplete student response—no sampling

A lot of 4th graders in my class spend their time after school first by doing homework, and then either go over friends house or play outside.

If I were to record my data I would make a tally chart.

Standard: Formulate questions that can be addressed with data and collect, organize, and display relevant data to answer them

Expectation: Represent data using tables and graphs such as line plots, bar graphs, and line graphs

---

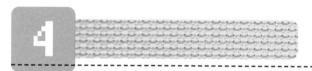

The students in Mr. Kirby's class voted for their favorite book of the past 3 months.

The three books that they read were these:

Babe, the Gallant Pig   **Sarah, Plain and Tall**   **Stone Fox**

Here are some clues about the results of the vote.

a. 34 students voted.
b. The winner got the most votes, but got fewer than half the votes.
c. There was a two-way tie for second place.

In the space below, make a chart or graph that shows voting results that fit all three clues.

Source: Balanced Assessment (http://balancedassessment.concord.org)
About the mathematics: This item involves the use of part-whole information to make a chart or graph while managing some constraints.
Solution: Answers will vary, but two correct representations are shown.

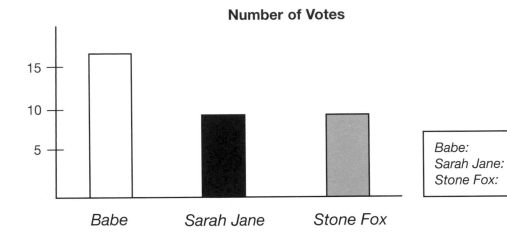

Number of Votes

Babe:	16
Sarah Jane:	9
Stone Fox:	9

Number of Votes

Babe:	12
Sarah Jane:	11
Stone Fox:	11

Rubric

- Meets standard
  - — All constraints in the clues are managed successfully.
  - — Voting result is organized clearly in a chart or table.
  - — Votes for each book may be shown as tallies or with the numerical total.
  - — Elements of the chart (i.e., number of votes, book title) are labeled.
  - — A clear and accurate graph is produced.
- Needs revision
  - — All the constraints contained are managed successfully.
  - — Chart or graph is not well organized or is difficult to follow.
- Needs instruction
  - — Two or three of the constraints in the clues are managed.
  - — The graph is poorly organized or hard to read.
  - — Calculation error may have been made in totaling the votes.
- Needs significant instruction
  - — One or no constraints in the clues are given.
  - — Chart may be difficult to read.

Student Work

Correct student responses

Responses 1 and 2 meet the standard of producing a clear and accurate graph. All constraints are managed successfully. The responses show the book titles and the votes counted for each one.

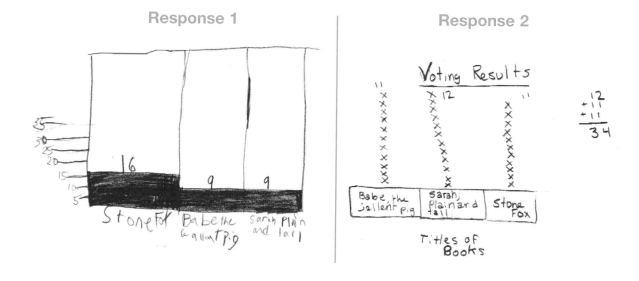

Response 1   Response 2

159

Partially correct student response

Needs revision. All constraints are managed, but no graph is produced. The results are difficult to follow.

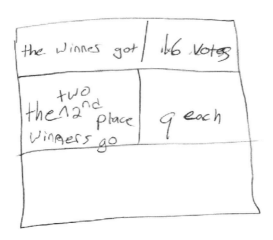

the winnes got | 16 votes

the 2nd two place winners go | 9 each

Incorrect student responses

Response 1

Needs instruction. The answer does not show that 34 students voted. The student does not manage the constraints accurately (the numerical values are incorrect).

Babe the Gallant Pig =
Babe
Sarah Plain and Tall =
Sarah
Stone Fox = Stone

16, 7, 7

Response 2

Needs instruction. The totals are incorrect, and the book titles are missing. The graph is difficult to interpret, and the numerical values are incorrect.

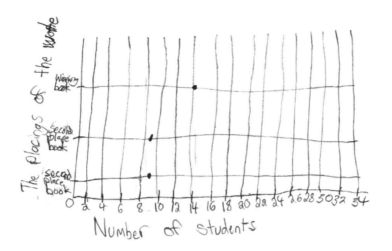

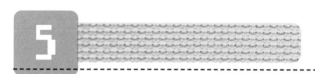

5

The data below show how students scored on last week's mathematics test:

Score	Number of Students
70	2
75	1
80	4
85	3
90	6
95	7
100	5

A. Make a line plot for these scores.
B. Four students were absent and took the test later. One student scored 60, two scored 90, and one student scored 95. Make a new line plot including the scores for these additional four students.
C. Compare the median and the mode for these two line plots. Describe similarities and differences.

About the mathematics: Students calculate measures of central tendency; select and use statistical methods to analyze data; develop and evaluate inferences that are based on data.

Solution

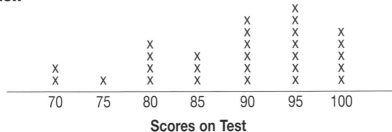

Scores on Test

Mode: 95
Median: 90

Scores on Test, Including Make-up Scores

Mode: 90 and 95
Median: 90

Both medians are the same; however, the modes changed when the additional student test scores were added. The mode changed from 95 to two modes of 90 and 95.

Rubric

Points Possible	Description	Points Awarded
2	One graph shows values from the table. The second graph shows the five added values.	
2	Median found for each graph. Median of first graph is 90; median of second graph is 90.	
1	Notes that the medians in both graphs are the same. Median did not change when scores were added.	
2	Mode found for each graph. Mode of first graph is 95, and second graph has two modes (i.e., is bimodal), 90 and 95	
1	Notes that the first graph has one mode and that the second graph has two modes.	

The 4th graders and 3rd graders in San Diego planted some fast-growing plants. The charts below show the results for the plants in the 4th-grade class and the results for the plants in the 3rd-grade class.

A. Make line plots for the 4th-grade results and the 3rd-grade results shown below. Organize the data on two line plots.

4th Grade	
Plant Height in cm	Number of Plants
9	/
14	/
17	/
22	/
23	/
25	/
26	/
27	///
28	/
29	//
30	/
31	///
32	/
33	//
35	/
39	/
40	/

3rd Grade	
Plant Height in cm	Number of Plants
15	/
20	////
22	//
23	̶H̶I̶ /
40	/

B. Describe the shape and important features of the line plots:
   • What is different about the two line plots?
   • What is the same for the two line plots?
   • Compare the median of both sets of data. What conclusions can you make?
   • How else can you describe the data?

Source: Adapted from *Principles and Standards for School Mathematics* (NCTM 2000, p. 180, question 1)

About the mathematics: Students select and use appropriate statistical methods to analyze data, develop and evaluate inferences, and make predictions that are based on data.

Solution

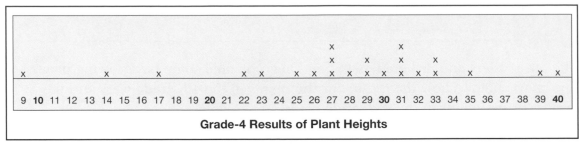

Grade-4 Results of Plant Heights

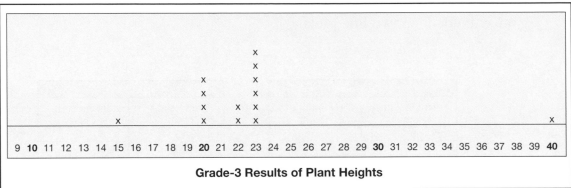

Grade-3 Results of Plant Heights

The data in the grade-4 line plot are more spread out than the grade-3 data. The grade-3 data cluster around 22 to 23 centimeters. The observations for grade 4 span from 9 to 40 centimeters (range of 31). The grade-3 observations span from 15 to 40 centimeters (range of 25). The tallest plant height in both grades was 40 centimeters, but grade 4 had the shortest plant height, 9 centimeters. The median plant height for grade 4 was 29 centimeters, and the mode was both 27 and 31 centimeters. For grade 3, the median plant height was 22.5 centimeters and the mode was 23 centimeters.

Because so many of the grade-4 plants grew higher than the grade-3 plants, grade 4 may have had seeds for taller plants. Grade 4 may also have used more fertilizer, or its plants may have had better soil, better light, or more water than those in grade 3. One plant in grade 3 seems different from the others. Perhaps that plant was grown from a seed from the grade-4 packet.

Most of the grade-4 plant heights were in the range of 22 to 33 centimeters, whereas the grade-3 plant heights were between 20 and 23 centimeters.

Rubric

Points Possible	Description	Points Awarded
2	Correctly displays data for 4th grade and for 3rd grade in line plots	
1	Notes differences (e.g., the 4th-grade plants grew taller, the shortest plant for 4th grade was 9 cm but for 3rd grade was 15 cm, the 4th-grade plants had a larger range of growth)	
1	Notes similarities (e.g., each grade had a plant that grew to a height of 40 centimeters).	
1	Finds medians of both graphs. The median for 3rd grade is 22.5, and the median for 4th grade is 29.	
2	Draws conclusions (e.g., may conclude that 3rd and 4th graders had different plants, that 4th graders had more light or water or fertilizer or better seeds, that one 3rd grader had a 4th-grade seed)	
1	Describes the data in alternative ways (e.g., lists multiple differences, similarities, or conclusions)	

Standard: Formulate questions that can be addressed with data and collect, organize, and display relevant data to answer them

Expectation: Recognize the differences in representing categorical and numerical data

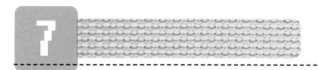

Determine whether the data listed are categorical (C) or numerical (N).

a. Lengths of students' strides
b. Students' eye color
c. Students' heights
d. Students' arm spans

e. Type of zoo animals
f. Students' weights at birth
g. Crayon colors
h. Favorite holidays

Source: Adapted from *Navigating through Data Analysis and Probability in Grades 3–5* (Chapin et al. 2002, p. 19)
About the mathematics: This item involves determining the nature of data.
Solution: a. N; b. C; c. N; d. N; e. C; f. N; g. C; h. C

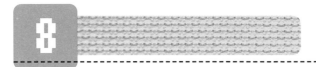

From the list below, name the best type of graph that you might use to record the following data. Explain why.

bar graph　　line graph　　line plot　　circle graph

A. The favorite food for your class
B. Temperature change over a 24-hour period
C. Weights of players on a football team
D. Choices for school colors

About the mathematics: Students select appropriate graphical representation for data.

Solution: A. Line plot, bar graph, or circle graph; both a bar graph and a line plot would show how many students liked a particular food, and a circle graph would show the percent of students who liked a particular food. B. Line graph; a line graph is a good illustration of change over time. C. Line plot, bar graph, or circle graph; both a line plot and a bar graph would show how many players weigh a certain amount, and a circle graph would show the percent of players at certain weights. D. Line plot, bar graph, or circle graph; both a line plot and a bar graph would show the number of students who chose certain colors, and a circle graph would show the percent of students choosing certain colors.

Standard: Select and use appropriate statistical methods to analyze data

Expectation: Describe the shape and important features of a set of data and compare related data, with an emphasis on how the data are distributed

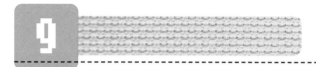

Sue and Jill made bar graphs to show what kind of pizza their class liked. The data are given here:

Pepperoni	16
Pineapple	7
Mushroom	10

Sue made her graph with intervals of 1, and Jill made her graph with intervals of 5. Why do these two graphs of the same data look different?

Sue's Graph

Jill's Graph

Intervals of 1:

Intervals of 5:

Teacher note: A change in the interval changes the perception of the information in the graph. Graphs can be made to persuade the consumer.

About the mathematics: The explanation involves noting similarities and differences between two data sets, requiring students to become more precise in their description of data.

Solution: The explanation should address issues of scale, that is, if the axis is marked off by 1's, a bar of height 10 will appear much taller than if the axis is marked off by 5's.

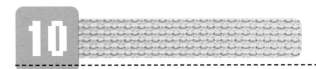

The line plot below shows how students scored on last week's mathematics test.

```
                                        x
                                        x               x
                                        x               x       x
                                        x               x       x
                        x       x       x       x       x       x
                x       x       x       x       x       x       x
        x       x       x       x       x       x       x       x

        60      65      70      75      80      85      90      95      100
```

A. How many students scored 90 or higher on the test?
B. What is the difference between the highest score and the lowest score?
C. How many students scored less than 70?

About the mathematics: The solution involves interpreting and analyzing graphical data.

Solution: A. 14 students; B. 40 is the difference between the highest and lowest scores; C. 3 students

Standard: Select and use appropriate methods to analyze data

Expectation: Use measures of center focusing on the median, and understand what each does and does not indicate about the data set

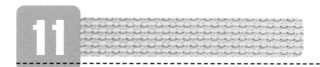

11

The table below shows the number of minutes that seven students spent on their mathematics homework yesterday.

Student	Minutes Spent on Homework
Sean	34
Amanda	25
Ben	40
Mike	20
Shannon	32
Steve	25
Rachel	27

On the basis of the information in the table, what is the median number of minutes the seven students spent on their mathematics homework?

> **About the mathematics:** Students identify the median in a set of data.
> **Solution:** 27 minutes

12

The graph below shows how many of the 32 children in Mr. Rivera's class are 8, 9, 10, and 11 years old. Which of the following is true?

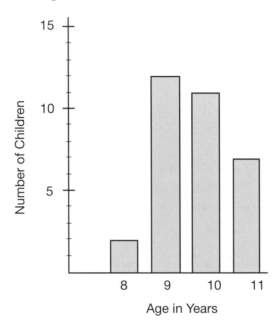

Ages of Children In Mr. Rivera's Class

a. Most are younger than 9.
b. Most are younger than 10.
c. Most are 9 or older.
d. None of the above is true.

Source: National Assessment of Educational Progress (1992, block 4M7, item 3)

About the mathematics: The solution involves reading information from graphs.

Solution: c

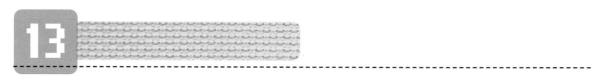

Each boy and girl in the class voted for his or her favorite kind of music. Here are the results.

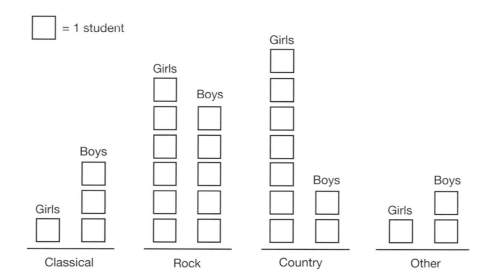

Which kind of music did most students in the class prefer?

a. Classical
b. Rock
c. Country
d. Other

How do you know?

Source: Adapted from National Assessment of Educational Progress (1996, block 4M12, item 4)

About the mathematics: Students propose and justify conclusions based on data.

Solution: b. Rock. It has the highest frequency (11) of the four categories.

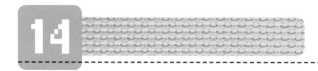

FINAL TEST SCORES	
Score	Number of Students
95	50
90	120
85	170
80	60
75	10

Use the information in the table above to complete the bar graph below.

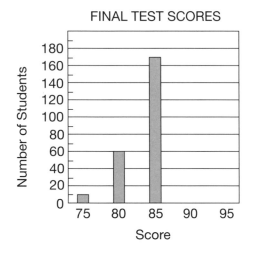

Source: National Assessment of Educational Progress (2003, block 4M6, item 6)

About the mathematics: This item requires students to represent data using tables and graphs.

Solution: 90 and 95 are correctly drawn on the graph. See the student work that follows.

Student Work

Correct student response	Incorrect student response

FINAL TEST SCORES

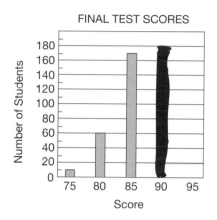

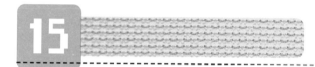

15

The Padres Baseball team recorded the number of home runs for last season for their top hitters.

41, 28, 28, 34, 49

A. What is the mean number of home runs for last season? How do you know?

B. Unfortunately, two players accidentally got left off the list. When their data were included, the mean changed. Klesko hit 58 home runs, and Nevin hit 52 home runs. Will the new mean be higher, be lower, or stay the same? Explain

> **Teacher note:** This item could be adapted to find the median and then the change in the median.
>
> **About the mathematics:** This item involves using the mean, a measure of central tendency, and comparing the effect of additional data on the mean.
>
> **Solution**
>
> A. The mean number of homeruns is 36. How do you know? The total number of homeruns (41 + 28 + 28 + 34 + 49) divided by 5 (number of hitters) is 36.
>
> B. Mean number of homeruns is now 41 3/7, or 41.428. We know that the mean will be higher because the two additional players each had more than 36 home runs.

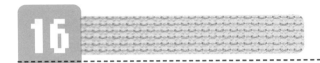

Morris Elementary School is selling candy bars to raise money for sports equipment. The table below shows the number of candy bars sold in one week.

Day	Sun	Mon	Tues	Weds	Thurs	Fri	Sat
Candy	31	18	18	15		23	31

Corey got ketchup on his data table and can not read Thursday's candy count, but he knows two things:

a. He knows that the median is 18.
b. He knows that Thursday's candy count was not 18.

1. What might Thursday's candy count have been so that the median is 18? Explain.
2. Saturday's count was a mistake. It is supposed to be 41. Does this correction change the median? Why or why not?

About the mathematics: This item focuses on the median as a measure of center.

Solution

a. Any number 17 or less, otherwise 18 will not be in the middle. (The answer can list the values and show how a number less than 17 will give the middle number.)
b. No, replacing a number on the end does not change anything.

Rubric

Proficient: Puts numbers in order from smallest to largest and shows evidence of selecting numbers that will work.

Developing: Puts numbers in order from smallest to largest and uses trial and error until arriving at correct answer.

Beginning: May or may not put numbers in order from smallest to largest. Shows an incorrect or strategy and arrives at an incorrect solution

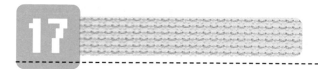

Leon has taken 9 math quizzes this year. His quiz scores are shown below.

| 98 | 90 | 76 | 88 | 82 | 100 | 75 | 85 | 75 |

a. What is the median of Leon's math quiz scores? How do you know?
b. What is the mode of Leon's math quiz scores? Show your work, or explain your answer.
c. Which number better represents the scores that Leon has received, the mode or the median? Justify your choice.

About the mathematics: This item involves identifying median and mode in a data set.

Solution

a. The median is 85. Put the numbers in order from smallest to largest, and find the number in the middle.
b. The mode is 75 because 75 appears twice, which is more often than any other score appears.
c. He should use the median because in this instance the mode also represents his lowest score, whereas he scored higher than 75 on seven of the tests. The median is better than the mode for representing the scores that Leon has received.

Rubric

Points Possible	Description	Points Awarded
Part a: 1	Correctly finds the median.	
Part a: 1	Justifies answer by appropriate methods, e.g., by putting numbers in order from smallest to largest to find the median	
Part b: 1	Correctly finds the mode	
Part c: 2	Correctly identifies the median as the better representation for the scores and provides justification	

Standard: Select and use appropriate statistical methods to analyze data

Expectation: Compare different representations of the same data and evaluate how well each representation shows important aspects of the data

18

One hundred eighty 5th graders were asked to choose an activity to be a part of the after-school activities. The same data are shown on two different graphs.

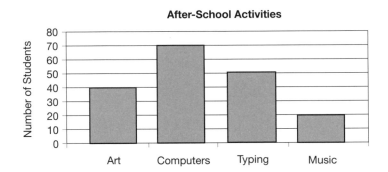

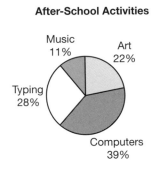

a. What information does the bar graph tell you that the circle graph does not?
b. If the budget for after-school activities was $500.00, which graph would you use to decide how much money to give to each program. Why?

> **About the mathematics:** This item requires students to compare multiple representations of the same data.

Solution

a. The bar graph tells—
  * the total number of students;
  * the number of students in each activity.

b. The pie graph because—
  * you can find 39 percent of $500 and give it to the computer activity (for example);
  * music plus computers equals 50 percent, so those two programs should get half the money.

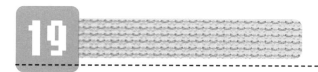

The high temperatures for the week have been organized in a bar graph. Create another type of graph to represent the high temperatures. Which graph better represents the data, and why?

High Temperatures for the Week

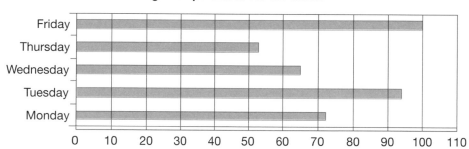

About the mathematics: This item requires comparing multiple representations of the same data.

Solution: Answers will vary on the basis of the other graph created by the student.

Standard: Develop and evaluate inferences and predictions that are based on data

Expectation: Propose and justify conclusions and predictions that are based on data and design studies to further investigate the conclusions or predictions

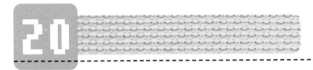

There is only one red marble in each of the bags shown below. Without looking, you are to pick a marble out of one of the bags.

A. Which bag would give you the greatest chance of picking the red marble? How do you know?
B. Which bag would give the least chance of picking the red marble? How do you know?

a. Bag with 10 marbles
b. Bag with 100 marbles
c. Bag with 1000 marbles
d. It makes no difference.

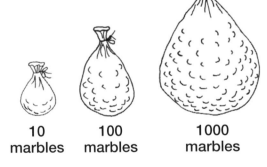

10
marbles

100
marbles

1000
marbles

Source: Adapted from National Assessment of Educational Progress (2003, grade 4, block 4M10, item 16)

About the mathematics: Students understand and apply basic concepts of probability; they also describe events and make a prediction.

Solution

Part A: The answer is a. The justification includes the following:

- The greatest chance is the smallest bag, with 10 marbles. Every bag contains 1 red marble, and this bag has only 10 marbles; so the probability of getting a red marble is $^1/_{10}$.

Part B: The answer is c. The justification includes the following:

- The least chance is the largest bag, with 1,000 marbles. It contains 1 red marble among 1000 marbles, so the probability of getting a red marble is only $^1/_{1000}$.

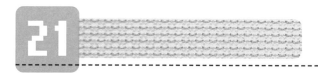

Chase's fifth-grade class used a spinner with 5 equal sections like the one shown below to do an experiment in class.

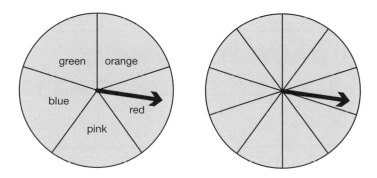

The students are making a new spinner with 10 equal sections. For the 10-section spinner, the arrow has to have the same probability of landing on red as with the 5-section spinner.

What is the total number of sections that must be marked red on the new spinner?

a. 1
b. 2
c. 4
d. 5

About the mathematics: For an equally likely outcome, the chances to land on the desired outcome must be proportional. The first spin will produce a 1-in-5 chance, but because the second spin is independent of the first spin, the number of outcomes and the number of possible outcomes doubles.
Solution: b

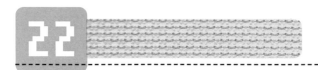

The bar graph shows the lengths of the hiking trails at Cowles Mountain Trails. Use the graph to answer the questions below.

Cowles Mountain Hiking Trails

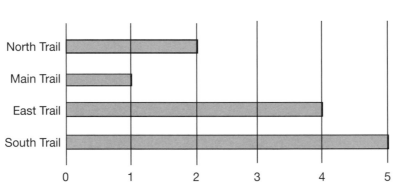

A. Which trail is longer than 3 miles but shorter than 5 miles?
   a. North Trail
   b. Main Trail
   c. East Trail
   d. South Trail

B. Melissa hiked two of the trails on Saturday. She walked six miles altogether. Which two trails could she have hiked?
   a. Main and South
   b. North and Main
   c. South and North
   d. East and Main

About the mathematics: This item involves interpreting data presented in a bar graph.

Solution

    A. c, East Trail

    B. a, Main and South

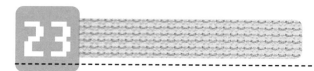

23

Students at Crawford Elementary School rode bikes to raise money for field trips. Carmen made this graph showing the records of the top five bikers in the bike-a-thon.

Number of Miles Biked in the Bike-a-thon

Carmen	🚲	🚲	🚲	🚲				
Lauren	🚲	🚲	🚲	🚲	🚲	🚲		
Marcus	🚲	🚲	🚲	🚲	🚲	🚲	🚲	🚲
Monica	🚲	🚲	🚲	🚲	🚲			
Mark	🚲	🚲	🚲					

Each 🚲 = $\frac{1}{2}$ mile.

A. Who biked more than 3 miles?

B. How many more miles did Lauren bike than Mark?

C. What is the median number of miles biked?

    a. $2\frac{1}{2}$

    b. 8

    c. 4

    d. $3\frac{1}{2}$

About the mathematics: The solution requires students to interpret data represented in a graph.
Solution: A. Marcus; B. one and a half miles; C. a, 2 $\frac{1}{2}$

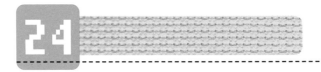

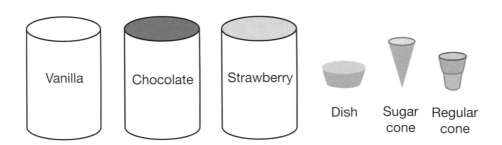

Jan's Snack Shop has 3 flavors of ice cream—vanilla, chocolate, and strawberry. The ice cream can be served in a dish, a sugar cone, or a regular cone. There are 9 people who choose 1 dip of ice cream in a dish, or in a sugar cone, or in a regular cone, and all of their choices are different.

a. List or show the 9 different choices.
b. Could another person have a choice that is different from one of these 9 choices? Why or why not?

Source: Adapted from National Assessment of Educational Progress (2003, grade 4, block 4M10, item 17)
About the mathematics: Students are asked to identify and verify all possible outcomes of a simple experiment and provide a representation of the data.

Solution: No more than nine choices are possible.

Students could make a list or a tree:

Vanilla	Chocolate	Strawberry
Dish	Dish	Dish
Sugar cone	Sugar cone	Sugar cone
Regular cone	Regular cone	Regular cone

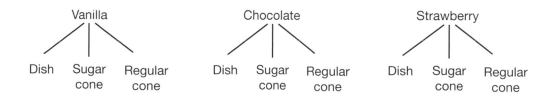

No, another person could not have a unique choice, because only 9 unique combinations are possible.

Student Work

Correct student response

Part a

① Vanilla and dish
② Vanilla and Sugar cone
③ Vanilla and regular cone
④ chocolate and dish
⑤ chocolate and sugar cone
⑥ chocolate and regular cone
⑦ strawberry and dish
⑧ strawberry and sugar cone
⑨ Strawberry and regular cone

Part b

No, they couldn't. Those are all the choices possible. If they ordered 2 scoops or if they combined them they could, but if they won a dip, those are all the possible choices.

Partially correct student response

Part a

1 Vanilla with a dish
2 chocolate with a sugar cone
3 strawberry with a Regular cone
4 Vanilla with a sugar cone
5 Chocolate with a regular cone
6 Strawberry with a dish

Minimal student response

Part a

strawberry

chocolate

vanilla

dish

sugar cone

regular cone

Incorrect student response

Part a

dish
sugar cone
regular cone

Part b

no, because you can't have
both

Standard: Understand and apply basic concepts of probability

Expectation: Describe events as likely or unlikely and discuss the degree of likelihood using such words as *certain, equally likely,* and *impossible*

25

On the swim team are 3 fifth graders and 2 sixth graders. Everyone's name is put in a hat, and the captain is chosen by picking one name. What are the chances that the captain will be a fifth grader? Is it likely?

Explain your answer.

Source: Adapted from National Assessment of Educational Progress (1996, block 4M9, item 9)

About the mathematics: This item requires students to predict the likelihood of a selection from a data set.

Solution: Five names are in the hat, and 3 of them are fifth graders' names. So among the 5 names, 3 possibilities exist that the draw will be a fifth grader's name: $3/5$. Yes, it is likely.

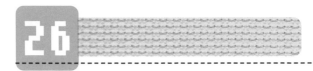

26

The 16 stickers listed below are placed in a box. If one sticker is drawn from the box, which color is it most likely to be?

Stickers	Number
Red	///
Blue	////
Yellow	//
Green	~~////~~ //

a. Red
b. Blue
c. Yellow
d. Green

Source: National Assessment of Educational Progress (1990, grade 4, block 4M7, item 4)
About the mathematics: Students are required to predict an event as likely or not likely.
Solution: d, Green

27

Stacia made a hundreds chart like the one on the following page on a piece of paper so that the entire sheet was covered. Then she shut her eyes and put her finger on the chart.

A. Is it more likely that she put her finger on a one-digit number or a two-digit number?
B. Is it more likely that she put her finger on an even number or an odd number?

Explain how you know.

0	1	2	3	4	5	6	7	8	9
10	11	12	13	14	15	16	17	18	19
20	21	22	23	24	25	26	27	28	29
30	31	32	33	34	35	36	37	38	39
40	41	42	43	44	45	46	47	48	49
50	51	52	53	54	55	56	57	58	59
60	61	62	63	64	65	66	67	68	69
70	71	72	73	74	75	76	77	78	79
80	81	82	83	84	85	86	87	88	89
90	91	92	93	94	95	96	97	98	99

Teacher note: Some students may be unaware that zero is considered even. This problem may raise discussion about that fact.

About the mathematics: The ratio of the number of outcomes to the number of possible outcomes is clear in this problem. The fraction (two-digit numbers)/(possible numbers) is very close to 1, which represents a highly likely event.

Solution

    A. Her finger is more likely to fall on a two-digit number, because the chart contains 90 two-digit numbers and only 10 one-digit numbers.

    B. The chances are equally likely that her finger will fall on an even number as on an odd number, because the chart contains 50 even numbers and 50 odd numbers.

Or:

    A. The chances are more likely that she put her finger on a two-digit number, because so many more two-digit numbers than one-digit numbers appear in the chart.

    B. The chances are equally likely that she put her finger on an even number as on an odd number, because the chart has equally many odd and even numbers.

Standard: Understand and apply basic concepts of probability

Expectation: Predict the probability of outcomes of simple experiments and test the predictions

28

The balls in this picture are placed in a box, and a child picks one without looking.

a. What is the probability that the ball picked will be the one with dots?
b. What is the probability that the ball picked will have stripes?
c. What is the probability that the ball picked will not have stripes?
d. What is the probability that the ball will not have dots?

Source: Adapted from National Assessment of Educational Progress (2003, block 4M7, item 10)
About the mathematics: Students are asked to predict the probability of outcomes of simple experiments.
Solution
   a. $^1/_4$
   b. $^2/_4$
   c. $^2/_4$
   d. $^3/_4$

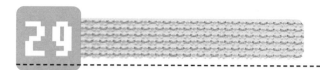

A fair coin is flipped five times. The results, in order, are tails, tails, heads, heads, and tails. If the coin is tossed again, what is the chance that the result will be tails?

a. 1 out of 3
b. 1 out of 2
c. 1 out of 5
d. No chance

About the mathematics: Students are asked to determine the probability of outcomes in a simple experiment. Probability is determined by the fraction

$$\frac{\textbf{number of favorable outcomes}}{\textbf{number of possible outcomes}}.$$

Students will want to rely on patterns or explain probability by saying, "That number already came up a lot." Because one coin is involved, only two different outcomes are possible. Each toss of the coin is independent of the next toss, so *every time* you flip the coin, you have an equally likely chance of getting tails or heads: one out of two.

Solution: b, 1 out of 2

30

Bill is rolling a fair number cube with faces numbered 1 through 6. What is the probability that the result on his next roll will be an even number? How do you know?

About the mathematics: Probability is determined by the fraction

$$\frac{\textbf{number of favorable outcomes}}{\textbf{number of possible outcomes}}.$$

The even outcomes are 2, 4, and 6; and the odd outcomes are 1, 3, and 5. Set up the ratio (three possible outcomes)/(six total outcomes). Students may also start to realize that they have an equally likely chance of rolling an odd number as an even number and that equally likely chances between two sets would be $^1/_2$.

Solution: $^1/_2$ or $^3/_6$

31

Luis wants to pick two marbles from a bag of red marbles and green marbles. One possible result is one red marble first and one green marble second. He wrote this result in the chart below. List all the other possible results that Luis could get.

R stands for one red marble.
G stands for one green marble.

First marble	Second marble
R	G

About the mathematics: This item involves creating an organized list of all possible outcomes (called the *sample space*).
Solution: RG, RR, GR, GG

The gum ball machine has 100 gum balls; 20 are yellow, 30 are blue, and 50 are red. The gum balls are well mixed inside the machine. Jenny gets 10 gum balls from this machine. What is your best prediction of the number that will be red?

20 yellow
30 blue
50 red

Explain why you chose this number.

Source: Adapted fom National Assessment of Educational Progress (1996, block 4M12, item 9)

About the mathematics: This item requires students to determine the probability of the outcome of a simple experiment.

Solution: 5 gum balls; see student work.

Student Work

Correct student responses

Response 1

Answer: ___5___ gum balls

Explain why you chose this number.

It is half of ten

Response 2

Answer: _5_ gum balls

Explain why you chose this number.

because red has the biggest number 50 and 10 ÷ 2 is 5 so 30 + 20 = 50 and the rest would be blue and yellow

Response 3

Answer: _5_ gum balls

Explain why you chose this number.

Be cause there are more red gum balls. Also because there are 50 red gumballs, 20 yellow gumballs and 30 blue gumbal

Response 4

Answer: _6_ gum balls

Explain why you chose this number.

I got that answer because these are more reds so more chances of getting it.

Partially correct student responses

Response 1

Answer: ___6___ gum balls

Explain why you chose this number.

because. There are 50 red. 20 are yellow 30 are blue.

Response 2

Answer: ___5___ gum balls

Explain why you chose this number.

I picked that one because I wanted to put the number that was infront the 0.

Minimal student responses

Response 1

Answer: __red__ gum balls

Explain why you chose this number.

Red has the most the most colored gum balls

Response 2

Answer: ___50___ gum balls

Explain why you chose this number.

Because Their are more red Gum Balls

Incorrect student responses

Response 1

Answer: *2 red* gum balls

Explain why you chose this number.

The average number of gum balls is 100 there is only 2 ways you can get 1— "red" because it is well mixed.

Response 2

Answer: *40* gum balls

Explain why you chose this number.

becase if she got 10 red that makes 10 less then have 40.

Standard: Understand and apply basic concepts of probability

Expectation: Understand that the measure of the likelihood of an event can be represented by a number from 0 to 1

33

Consider the following list of events. Describe each of the following as *certain, likely, unlikely,* or *impossible.*

a. Take 2 cubes, each with the numbers 1, 2, 3, 4, 5, and 6 written on its six faces. Throw them at random, and the sum of the numbers on the top face is less than or equal to 12.

b. New Year's Day falls on January 1.

c. The likelihood that a flipped coin will land "heads up"

d. A sports game is played somewhere in this country on any Sunday in July

e. When it is sunny, it rains.

f. Pick any two one-digit numbers, and their sum is 19.

g. You will be older tomorrow.

h. The likelihood that the next baby born in a nearby hospital will be a boy.

Which of the events has a probability close to or equal to 0?

Which of the events has a probability close to or equal to $1/2$?

Which of the events has a probability close to or equal to 1?

> **About the mathematics:** Impossible events have a probability of 0, certain-to-happen events have a probability of 1, and all other probabilistic events have a probability between 0 and 1.
>
> **Solution:** Choices e and f have probability close to or equal to 0. Choices a, b, d, and g have probability close to or equal to 1. Choices c and h have a probability close to or equal to $1/2$.
>
> a. certain
> b. certain
> c. likely
> d. likely/certain
> e. unlikely
> f. impossible
> g. certain
> h. likely

Professional Development

EXAMINING student work is an established effective professional development strategy for enhancing teacher practice. Teachers who examine student work have opportunities to gain valuable insights to influence their instructional practice. They can learn whether their students are acquiring important mathematical ideas and how better to help students develop an understanding of important mathematical concepts. Preservice teachers may also gain valuable insights into how children think and reason about mathematics if they have opportunities to examine student work. Guided discussion about student responses and suggestions for how best to address student misconceptions in a classroom setting are beneficial to those preparing to teach mathematics to young children.

Consider, for example, students' responses to the following question.

> **What is the quickest way to solve the problem 12 × 25?**
>   **A**   **Mental computation**
>   **B.**   **Estimation**
>   **C.**   **Paper and pencil**
>   **D.**   **Calculator**
> **Why? Explain your thinking.**

Student Thinking and Instructional Insights

The student work we obtained from this item was very interesting, and we have included examples for each of the distractors. The choice of calculator was by far the most popular choice. In examining this work, teachers might engage in a discussion about how best to empower students to use number sense to solve a computation. It might also prompt a discussion about when calculator use is appropriate. Because this particular item asked students for the quickest way to "solve" the problem, estimation is not a correct answer. Discussion about when and how best to estimate an answer is important for teachers to promote, especially because many students confuse estimation with rounding.

The reasons that students 1 and 2 chose "mental computation" are very enlightening. Student 1 shows development of number sense and ability to decompose a problem to obtain an answer. Student 2 indicates a similar development of number sense but has decomposed the problem differently. Both students demonstrate strong number sense.

Student 1

Why?

Mental computation because you know that 4x25 equals 100, so if 4 goes into 12 three times, the answer is three times 100 which is 300.

Student 2

Ⓐ Mental computation
Why?

First you multiply 25x10=250. then you multiply 2x25=50. 25+50=300

Students 3 and 4 incorrectly choose "estimation" as the quickest way to *solve* the problem. Both seem to look at estimation as a quick way to get about the right answer. Perhaps they misread the directions and did not realize that they were being asked to find a way to solve the problem. Follow-up questions would reveal more information about these students' thinking. However, the distinction between when to estimate and when to solve would be appropriate instruction for both.

Student 3

(B) Estimation
Why?

Because you don't have to tipe any thing in and you don't have to write any complicated number problems. You just round it off and add in the other numbers in the end.

Student 4

(B.) Estimation
Why?

I think its faster to do the problem is to estimate because you will have about the same answer and not have to take time on figureing it out.

Students 5 and 6 chose paper and pencil. Student 5 appears to be referring to an algorithm for multiplication. This student also demonstrates an awareness of the relationship between multiplication and division. Student 6 shows great confidence in the outcome of a competition between one's own "brain" and the calculator.

Student 5

(C) Paper and pencil

Why?

> You can do it like this $\begin{matrix} 25 \\ \times 2 \end{matrix}$ and you can get the exact answer. If you don't think it look right you can check it with divison.

Student 6

(C) Paper and pencil

Why?

> Paper and pencil will be quiker because your brain is smater than a calculator and it will help you learn.

Students 7 and 8 both chose the calculator, and interestingly, both of them refer to writing the problem as being more time-consuming or more difficult than typing it. Student 8 provides a rationale for the choice made and even includes an explanation as to why estimation is not appropriate.

Student 7

(D.) Calculator
Why?

_Because calculators are never
wrong and they give the
correct answers. and it's
easier to type in and instead
of writing it_

Student 8

(D.) Calculator
Why?

_The calculator is the fastest way because
it takes a while to figure it out in your
head. Estimation isn't accurate, and it takes
a long time to write it down and
figure it out._

This sample of student work was chosen to show the wide variation in student thinking and insights that can be gained to help teachers make informed instructional decisions. Each student brings a unique perspective to the question, thus challenging the classroom teacher to provide a variety of experiences designed to engage all students in developing an understanding of the mathematics while addressing the misconceptions of some students.

Error Analysis

Examining student work can also provide the opportunity for "error analysis," that is, considering what misconceptions lie beneath incorrect, and sometimes correct, responses. Consider the following problem dealing with decimals:

> **Which is larger, 0.6 or 0.53? How do you know?**

Valuable discussion can occur about the reasons students give to justify their choice.

Consider these two typical responses:

> **Student 1: "0.53 is larger, since 53 is larger than 6."**
> **Student 2: "0.6 is larger, since hundredths are smaller than tenths."**

Which student is correct? Productive discussion emerges, and it clarifies the fact that although student 2 gives the correct answer, the reasoning is flawed. We could predict that student 2, if asked to order 0.95 and 0.4, would say that 0.95 is smaller because hundredths are smaller than tenths.

Considering student work can open up conversation among teachers about how such misconceptions may develop. For example, student 2 may have picked up on an overgeneralization to the effect that "the more places to the right of the decimal, the smaller the value gets." The student appears not to understand that although the value of the place (e.g., the hundredths or thousandths) gets smaller to the right of the decimal, the value of the digit in each place has an effect on the overall value of the number. The benefits of considering an example such as this for professional development are twofold: (a) it allows teachers to identify common misconceptions that students have about decimals, increasing the likelihood that the teacher will be able to target the specific misconception that a particular student may have, and (b) it allows teachers to consider carefully the kinds of justifications and statements made in class that can lead to students' misconceptions.

Problems with Multiple Correct Solutions

Some questions lend themselves well to consideration as a professional development topic because of the possibility of many correct solutions. Consider the following question, from the assessment items in chapter 3, "Geometry":

> **Use the trapezoid, the triangle, and the blue rhombus from your pattern blocks to complete parts A, B, and C of this question.**
>
> **A) Using all three blocks, create a parallelogram.**
>   **Trace your parallelogram in the space provided below.**
> **B) Using all three blocks, create a concave polygon.**
>   **Trace your concave polygon in the space provided below.**
> **C) Using all three blocks, create a pentagon.**
>   **Trace your pentagon in the space below.**

Finally, part D asks this:

> **Using any pattern blocks you wish, create a polygon so that all these conditions are satisfied:**
>
> **(i)   The number of yellow blocks used is one-half the number of red blocks.**
> **(ii) The final shape has only one line of reflective symmetry, and**
> **(iii) 8 blocks in total must be used.**

This four-part question raises many questions for the teacher.

Consider part A. Although teachers may easily recognize parallelograms, a more productive and challenging task is defining "parallelogram" and other familiar shapes (e.g., square, rectangle), not by looking up the terms in the textbook but by identifying the characteristics necessary for a shape to be a parallelogram (or square or rectangle.) In a professional development setting, teachers have the opportunity to refamiliarize themselves with such terminology as *concave* and *line of reflective symmetry*. Even a term such as *parallelogram* can lead to mathematical conversation when teachers are asked to define a parallelogram.

Regarding part D: although students are responsible for finding only one configuration that works, the extension of considering which combinations of blocks are possible can lead to fruitful discussion during professional development. Professional development can also provide time for teachers to consider the difference between a *line of reflective symmetry* and a *reflection of an object* in the plane. Another pair of terms that are sometimes confused are *rotation* and *rotational symmetry*. Having opportunities to consider these terms before teaching these topics allows teachers to anticipate potential student confusion and consider how to structure lessons to help students avoid confusion of these terms.

Conclusion

In summary, student work can be used in many ways for valuable professional development. Although only a few examples are discussed here, a limitless supply of fruitful examples is available from teachers' own classrooms. Examples pulled from teachers' classrooms are particularly effective for professional development when they form the basis for analysis of common work, that is, when all teachers participating in the professional development session bring in student responses to the same question or questions to lay the groundwork for the discussion.

Appendix
Items Matrices

Number and Operations Items Matrix, Chapter 1

Assessment Item Number	1	2	3	4	5	6	7	8	9	10	11	12	13	14	15	16	17	18	19	20	21	22	23
Standards and Expectations																							
Understand numbers, ways of representing numbers, relationships among numbers, and number systems																							
Understand the place-value structure of the base-ten number system and be able to represent and compare whole numbers and decimals	X	X	X																				
Recognize equivalent representations for the same number and generate them by decomposing and composing numbers				X																			
Develop understanding of fractions as parts of unit wholes, as parts of a collection, as locations on number lines, and as divisions of whole numbers					X	X	X	X	X														
Use models, benchmarks, and equivalent forms to judge the size of fractions										X	X	X	X	X	X								
Recognize and generate equivalent forms of commonly used fractions, decimals, and percents																X	X	X					
Explore numbers less than 0 by extending the number line and through familiar applications																			X	X			
Describe classes of numbers according to characteristics such as the nature of their factors																					X		X
Process Standards																							
Problem Solving															X						X	X	
Communication										X		X	X	X	X		X			X	X	X	
Reasoning and Proof						X	X					X	X	X	X	X	X		X				
Connections		X		X				X	X	X	X					X		X					X
Representation	X	X	X	X	X	X	X	X	X	X	X	X	X	X	X	X	X	X		X			X
Item Format	MC	SR	SR	MC	SR	SR	SR	SR	SR	MC/ER	SR	MC/ER	SR	MC	ER	MC	ER	SR	MC	ER	ER	ER	MC

Number and Operations Items Matrix, Chapter 1—Continued

Assessment Item Number	24	25	26	27	28	29	30	31	32	33	34	35	36	37	38	39	40	41	42
Standards and Expectations																			
Understand meanings of operations and how they relate to one another																			
Understand various meanings of multiplication and division	X	X																	
Understand the effects of multiplying and dividing whole numbers			X	X	X														
Identify and use relations between operations, such as division as the inverse of multiplication, to solve problems						X	X												
Understand and use properties of operations, such as the distributivity of multiplication over addition								X	X	X	X								
Compute fluently and make reasonable estimates																			
Develop fluency with basic number combinations for multiplication and division and use these combinations to mentally compute related problem, such as 30 X 50												X	X						
Develop fluency in adding, subtracting, multiplying, and dividing whole numbers														X	X	X	X		
Develop and use strategies to estimate the results of whole-number computations and to judge the reasonableness of such results																		X	X
Process Standards																			
Problem Solving						X			X	X	X	X				X	X		
Communication	X			X				X				X			X	X	X		
Reasoning and Proof		X			X	X		X			X		X	X	X	X	X	X	X
Connections	X		X	X			X		X	X	X		X	X	X	X		X	X
Representation	X		X	X			X		X	X	X	X		X	X	X	X		
Item Format	ER	SR	MC	ER	MC	SR	SR	ER	SR	SR	ER	MC	MC	SR	SR	ER	SR	MC	MC

Number and Operations Items Matrix, Chapter 1—*Continued*

Assessment Item Number	43	44	45	46	47	48	49	50	51
Standards and Expectations									
Compute fluently and make reasonable estimates									
Develop and use strategies to estimate computations involving fractions and decimals in situations relevant to students' experience	X	X	X	X					
Use visual models, benchmarks, and equivalent forms to add and subtract commonly used fractions and decimals					X	X			
Select appropriate methods and tools for computing with whole numbers from among mental computation, estimation, calculators, and paper and pencil according to the context and nature of the computation and use the selected method or tool							X	X	X
Process Standards									
Problem Solving			X			X			X
Communication			X	X	X	X	X	X	X
Reasoning and Proof			X		X	X	X	X	
Connections			X	X		X	X		
Representation			X	X	X	X			X
Item Format	ER	ER	ER	ER	ER	ER	ER	SR	ER

Algebra Items Matrix, Chapter 2

Assessment Item Number	1	2	3	4	5	6	7	8	9	10	11	12	13	14	15	16	17	18	19	20	21	22	23	24	25	26	27
Standards and Expectations																											
Understand patterns, relations, and functions																											
Describe, extend, and make generalizations about geometric and numeric patterns	X	X	X	X	X	X	X																				
Represent and analyze patterns and functions, using words, tables, and graphs								X	X	X	X	X															
Represent and analyze mathematical situations and structures using algebraic symbols																											
Identify such properties as commutativity, associativity, and distributivity and use them to compute with whole numbers													X	X	X												
Represent the idea of a variable as an unknown quantity using a letter or a symbol																X	X	X	X								
Express mathematical relationships using equations																				X	X	X	X				
Use mathematical models to represent and understand quantitative relationships																											
Model problem situations with objects and use representations such as graphs, tables, and equations to draw conclusions																								X	X	X	X
Process Standards																											
Problem Solving																	X	X	X					X			
Communication						X	X				X				X						X	X				X	X
Reasoning and Proof	X		X	X	X	X	X			X			X		X						X			X	X	X	
Connections		X						X	X	X	X	X		X				X	X	X	X		X		X		
Representation		X				X	X	X	X				X	X		X		X	X	X	X	X	X	X	X		
Item Format	SR	MC	SR	SR	SR	ER	ER	MC	SR	SR	SR	ER	SR	MC	MC/ER	MC	ER	MC	SR	MC	SR	ER	MC	ER	SR	ER	ER

Algebra Items Matrix, Chapter 2—Continued

Assessment Item Number	28	29	30	31	32	33	34	35
Standards and Expectations								
Analyze change in various contexts								
Investigate how a change in one variable relates to a change in a second variable	X	X	X	X	X	X	X	
Identify and describe situations with constant or varying rates of change and compare them								X
Process Standards								
Problem Solving					X			X
Communication		X			X			X
Reasoning and Proof	X		X	X	X	X	X	X
Connections	X	X		X				X
Representation	X	X	X	X	X	X	X	X
Item Format	MC	ER	SR	MC/ER	ER	SR	MC	ER

Geometry Items Matrix, Chapter 3

Assessment Item Number	1	2	3	4	5	6	7	8	9	10	11	12	13	14	15	16	17
Standards and Expectations																	
Analyze characteristics and properties of two- and three-dimensional geometric shapes and develop mathematical arguments about geometric relationships																	
Identify, compare, and analyze attributes of two-and three dimensional shapes and develop vocabulary to describe the attributes	X	X	X	X													
Classify two-and three-dimensional shapes according to their properties and develop definitions of classes of shapes such as triangles and pyramids					X	X	X										
Investigate, describe, and reason about the results of subdividing, combining, and transforming shapes								X	X	X							
Explore congruence and similarity											X						
Make and test conjectures about geometric properties and relationships and develop logical arguments to justify conclusions												X					
Specify locations and describe spatial relationships using coordinate geometry and other representational systems																	
Describe location and movement using common language and geometric vocabulary													X				
Make and use coordinate systems to specify locations and to describe paths														X	X	X	
Find the distance between points along horizontal and vertical lines of a coordinate system																	X
Process Standards																	
Problem Solving				X	X	X	X	X				X					
Communication		X	X	X	X	X	X	X	X		X	X					
Reasoning and Proof			X			X			X	X		X					
Connections	X												X	X			X
Representation	X	X	X	X	X	X	X	X	X	X	X	X	X	X	X	X	X
Item Format	MC	SR	SR	ER	ER	ER	ER	SR	MC	SR	MC	ER	SR	SR	SR	MC	SR

Geometry Items Matrix, Chapter 3—Continued

Assessment Item Number	18	19	20	21	22	23	24	25	26	27	28	29	30	31
Standards and Expectations														
Apply transformations and use symmetry to analyze mathematical situations														
Predict and describe the results of sliding, flipping, and turning two-dimensional shapes	X	X	X	X	X	X	X							
Describe a motion or a series of motions that will show that two shapes are congruent						X	X							
Identify and describe line and rotational symmetry in two and three-dimensional shapes and designs								X	X					
Use visualization, spatial reasoning, and geometric modeling to solve problems														
Build and draw geometric objects														
Create and describe mental images of objects, patterns, and paths										X				
Identify and build a three-dimensional object from two-dimensional representations of that object											X	X		
Identify and build a two-dimensional representation of a three-dimensional object														
Use geometric models to solve problems in other areas of mathematics, such as number and measurement														
Recognize geometric ideas and relationships and apply them to other disciplines and to problems that arise in the classroom or in everyday life													X	X
Process Standards														
Problem Solving	X	X	X	X									X	
Communication	X			X						X				X
Reasoning and Proof		X	X		X	X	X	X	X	X	X	X	X	
Connections			X		X				X	X	X	X	X	X
Representation	X	X	X	X	X		X	X	X		X		X	X
Item Format	MC	MC	MC	SR	MC	MC	MC	SR	SR	MC	MC	MC	MC	MC

Measurement Items Matrix, Chapter 4

Assessment Item Number	1	2	3	4	5	6	7	8	9	10	11	12	13	14	15	16	17	18	19	20	21	22	23	24	25	26
Standards and Expectations																										
Understand measurable attributes of objects and the units, systems, and processes of measurement																										
Understand such attributes as length, area, weight, volume, and size of angle and select the appropriate type of unit for measuring each attribute	X	X	X	X	X	X	X	X	X																	
Understand the need for measuring with standard units and become familiar with standard units in the customary and metric systems										X	X	X	X	X												
Carry out simple unit conversions, such as from centimeters to meters, within a system of measurement															X	X	X									
Understand that measurements are approximations and understand how differences in units affect precision																		X	X	X	X	X				
Explore what happens to measurements of a two-dimensional shape such as its perimeter and area when the shape is changed in some way																							X	X	X	X
Process Standards																										
Problem Solving																						X	X			
Communication						X	X	X	X	X	X	X	X	X			X	X	X	X	X		X	X	X	X
Reasoning and Proof													X	X		X	X	X	X	X	X	X		X	X	
Connections				X											X										X	
Representation	X		X		X	X	X		X	X	X	X	X	X												
Item Format	MC	SR	SR	MC	MC	SR	MC	ER	SR	SR	SR	MC	SR	MC/SR	SR	SR	ER	MC	MC	MC	SR	MC	ER	ER	MC	ER

Measurement Items Matrix, Chapter 4—Continued

Assessment Item Number	27	28	29	30	31	32	33	34	35	36	37	38	39	40	41	42	43
Standards and Expectations																	
Apply appropriate techniques, tools, and formulas to determine measurements																	
Develop strategies for estimating the perimeters, areas, and volumes of irregular shapes changed in some way	X	X	X	X	X												
Select and apply appropriate standard units and tools to measure length, area, volume, weight, time, temperature, and the size of angles						X	X	X	X	X	X	X					
Select and use benchmarks to estimate measurements													X	X			
Develop, understand, and use formulas to find the area of rectangles and related triangles and parallelograms															X	X	
Develop strategies to determine the surface areas and volumes of rectangular solids																	X
Process Standards																	
Problem Solving			X	X	X				X			X		X	X	X	X
Communication		X	X	X			X	X	X	X	X	X	X	X	X	X	
Reasoning and Proof		X	X	X			X	X		X	X	X	X	X	X	X	X
Connections						X				X	X						
Representation						X									X		
Item Format	SR	MC/SR	SR	ER	SR	MC	MC/SR	SR	SR	SR	SR	SR	SR	SR	SR	ER	MC/SR

Data Analysis and Probability Items Matrix, Chapter 5

Assessment Item Number	1	2	3	4	5	6	7	8	9	10	11	12	13	14	15	16	17	18	19
Standards and Expectations																			
Formulate questions that can be addressed with data and collect, organize, and display relevant data to answer them																			
Design investigations to address a question and consider how data-collection methods affect the nature of the data set	X																		
Collect data using observations, surveys, and experiments		X	X																
Represent data using tables and graphs such as line plots, bar graphs, and line graphs				X	X	X													
Recognize the differences in representing categorical and numerical data							X	X											
Select and use appropriate statistical methods to analyze data																			
Describe the shape and important features of a set of data and compare related data sets, with an emphasis on how the data are distributed									X	X									
Use measures of center, focusing on the median, and understand what each does and does not indicate about the data set											X	X	X	X	X	X	X		
Compare different representations of the same data and evaluate how well each representation shows important aspects of the data																		X	X
Process Standards																			
Problem Solving				X											X	X			X
Communication	X	X	X	X	X	X	X	X	X						X	X	X	X	X
Reasoning and Proof			X	X	X		X		X				X		X	X	X	X	
Connections		X	X	X						X		X		X					
Representation		X	X	X	X	X	X	X	X	X	X	X	X	X	X		X		X
Item Format	ER	MC/SR	ER	ER	ER	ER	SR	SR	ER	SR	SR	MC	MC/SR	SR	ER	ER	ER	ER	ER

Data Analysis and Probability Items Matrix, Chapter 5—*Continued*

Assessment Item Number	20	21	22	23	24	25	26	27	28	29	30	31	32	33
Standards and Expectations														
Develop and evaluate inferences and predictions that are based on data														
Propose and justify conclusions and predictions that are based on data and design studies to further investigate the conclusions or predictions	X	X	X	X	X									
Understand and apply basic concepts of probability														
Describe events as likely or unlikely and discuss the degree of likelihood using such words as *certain, equally likely,* and *impossible*						X	X	X						
Predict the probability of outcomes of simple experiments and test the predictions									X	X	X	X	X	
Understand that the measure of the likelihood of an event can be represented by a number from 0 to 1														X
Process Standards														
Problem Solving									X				X	
Communication			X		X	X		X					X	
Reasoning and Proof	X	X	X	X	X	X	X	X	X	X	X	X		X
Connections				X										
Representation	X	X		X	X			X	X			X		X
Item Format	MC/SR	MC	MC	SR	ER	SR	MC	ER	SR	MC	SR	SR	ER	SR

Bibliography

Balanced Mathematics Assessment for the Mathematics Curriculum. BA 18-02. Cambridge, Mass.: Harvard Graduate School of Education, 2002.

National Council of Teachers of Mathematics. *Curriculum and Evaluation Standards for School Mathematics.* Reston, Va.: National Council of Teachers of Mathematics, 1989.

————. *Principles and Standards for School Mathematics.* Reston, Va.: National Council of Teachers of Mathematics, 2000.

Schwartz, Judah, and Joan Kenney. *Balanced Mathematics Assessment for the 21st Century.* Cambridge, Mass.: Harvard Graduate School of Education, 2000.

Stenmark, Jean Kerr, ed. *Mathematics Assessment: Myths, Models, Good Questions, and Practical Suggestions.* Reston, Va.: National Council of Teachers of Mathematics, 1991.

Sources for Assessment Items

Balanced Assessment. http://balancedassessment.concord.org (accessed January 4, 2005)

Chapin, Suzanne, Alice Koziol, Jennifer MacPherson, and Carol Rezba. *Navigating through Data Analysis and Probability in Grades 3–5*, edited by Gilbert J. Cuevas and Peggy A. House. *Principles and Standards for School Mathematics* Navigations Series. Reston, Va.: National Council of Teachers of Mathematics, 2002.

Creative Publications. *Connect to NCTM Standards 2000.* Chicago: Creative Publications, 2000.

Curriculum Associates. *Comprehensive Assessment of Mathematic Strategies.* North Billerica, Mass.: 2000.

Exemplars: Standards-Based Performance Assessment and Instruction. http://www.exemplars.com/ (accessed January 4, 2005).

Greenes, Carole E., Carol R. Findell, M. Katherine Gavin, and Linda Jensen Sheffield. *Awesome Math Problems for Creative Thinking.* Chicago: Creative Publications, 2000.

Harcourt Math, Assessment Guide, Grade 4, California Edition, 2004. www.harcourtschool.com (accessed January 4, 2005).

Kentucky Department of Education. http://www.education.ky.gov (accessed January 4, 2005).

Lanius, Cynthia. Fun Mathematics Lesson. http://math.rice.edu/~lanius/Lessons (accessed January 4, 2005).

Massachusetts Department of Education. http://www.doe.mass.edu/mcas/testitems.html (accessed January 4, 2005).

National Assessment of Educational Progress. http://nces.ed.gov/nationsreportcard/ (accessed January 4, 2005).

National Council of Teachers of Mathematics. *Principles and Standards for School Mathematics.* Reston, Va.: National Council of Teachers of Mathematics, 2000.

New Standards Project. Available from Learning Research and Development Center, University of Pittsburgh, 3939 O'Hara Street, Pittsburgh, PA 15260.

Nova Scotia Department of Education. *Nova Scotia Elementary Mathematics Program Assessment.* Halifax: Nova Scotia Department of Education, 2003. http://plans.ednet.ns.ca/

Third International Mathematics and Science Study: United States. http://ustimss.msu.edu (accessed January 4, 2005).

Trends in International Mathematics and Science Study. http://nces.ed.gov/timss/ educators.asp (accessed January 4, 2005).

Virginia Department of Education http://www.pen.k12.va.us/ (accessed January 4, 2004).

Wilcox, Sandra K., Hugh Burkhardt, Phil Daro, Jim Ridgway, and Judah Schwartz. *Balanced Assessment for the Mathematics Curriculum.* Package 1. Palo Alto, Calif.: Dale Seymour Publications (Pearson Learning Group), 1999.

Wilcox, Sandra K., Hugh Burkhardt, Phil Daro, Jim Ridgway, Judah Schwartz, and Alan Schoenfeld. *Balanced Assessment for the Mathematics Curriculum.* Package 2. Palo Alto, Calif.: Dale Seymour Publications (Pearson Learning Group), 2000.

Three additional titles
are planned for the
Mathematics Assessment Samplers series

Anne M. Collins, series editor

⚙ *Mathematics Assessment Sampler, Prekindergarten–Grade 2: Items Aligned with NCTM's* Principles and Standards for School Mathematics,
edited by DeAnn Huinker

⚙ *Mathematics Assessment Sampler, Grades 6–8, Items Aligned with NCTM's* Principles and Standards for School Mathematics,
edited by John Burrill

⚙ *Mathematics Assessment Sampler, Grades 9–12, Items Aligned with NCTM's* Principles and Standards for School Mathematics,
edited by Betty Travis

Please consult www.nctm.org/catalog for the availability of these titles, as well as for a plethora of resources for teachers of mathematics at all grade levels.

For the most up-to-date listing of NCTM resources on topics of interest to mathematics educators, as well as information on membership benefits, conferences, and workshops, visit the NCTM Web site at www.nctm.org.